CW01642119

NORTH YORK MOORS
WEST A

Warne Gerrard Guides for Walkers

Walks for Motorists Series

CHESHIRE WALKS

COTSWOLDS WALKS
Northern
Southern

LAKE DISTRICT WALKS
Central
Northern
Western

LONDON COUNTRYSIDE WALKS
North West
North East
South West
South East

GREEN LONDON WALKS
(both circular and cross country)

MIDLAND WALKS

NORTH YORK MOORS WALKS
North and East
West and South

PEAK DISTRICT WALKS

PENDLESIDE AND BRONTE COUNTRY WALKS

YORKSHIRE DALES WALKS

FURTHER DALES WALKS

Long Distance and Cross Country Walks

WALKING THE PENNINE WAY

RAMBLES IN THE DALES

Warne Gerrard Guides for Walkers

NORTH YORK MOORS

WALKS FOR MOTORISTS

WEST AND SOUTH

Geoffrey White

Foreword by
John Hillaby

30 sketch maps
8 photographs

FREDERICK WARNE

Published by
Frederick Warne (Publishers) Ltd.
London

First published 1973
First revised edition 1975
Reprinted 1976
Second revised edition 1978

To my friend Geoffrey Green
my frequent and patient companion in the field.

The photograph on the front cover shows Yorkshire Wayfarers preparing to walk in the forest near Boltby. Reproduced by kind permission of the author. The photograph on the back cover shows the Kilburn White Horse. Reproduced by kind permission of the Yorkshire and Humberside Tourist Board.

All photographs and sketch maps by the author.
Sketches on pages 20 and 84 by Geoffrey Green,
remainder by the author.

ISBN 0 7232 2131 6

Printed by Galava Printing Co. Ltd., Nelson, Lancashire

Contents

SKETCHES

PHOTOGRAPHS

ACKNOWLEDGEMENT

The author wishes to thank Geoffrey Green and Norman Hancock for their assistance with this book.

GOING METRIC

The length of each walk in this book is given in miles and kilometres but within the text Imperial measurements are quoted. It is useful to bear the following approximations in mind:

5 miles = 8 km
½ mile = 805 metres
1 metre = 39.4 ins.

PLEASE LET US KNOW

Every care has been taken in the compilation of this book and the publishers cannot accept responsibility for any inaccuracies. But things change; paths are sometimes diverted: concrete bridges replace wooden ones: stiles disappear. Please let the publishers know if you discover anything like this on your way.

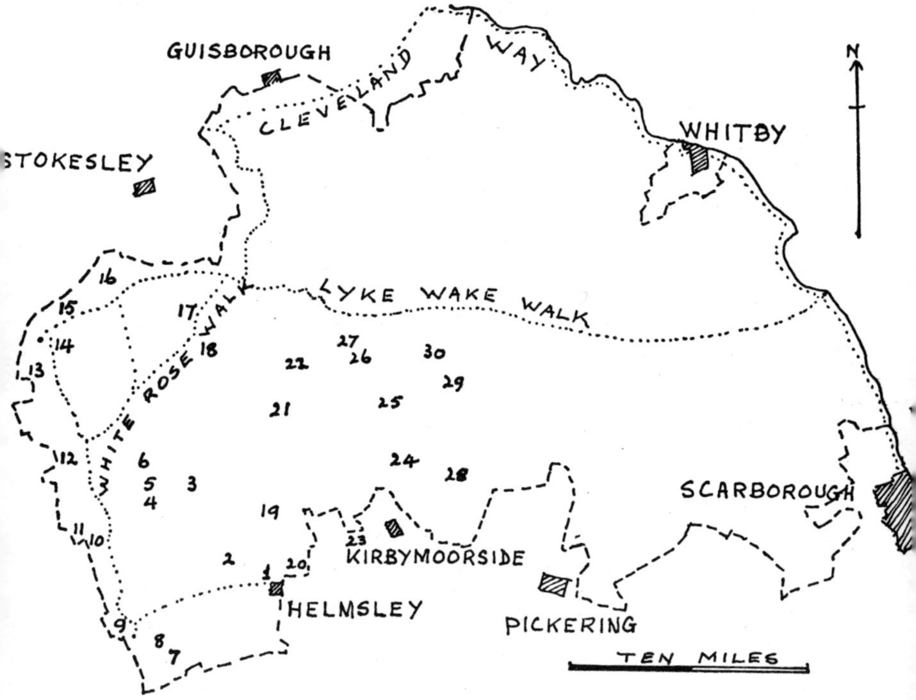

------ NATIONAL PARK BOUNDARY

NUMBERS DENOTE WALK START POINTS

The Publishers are grateful to Mr. JOHN HILLABY for writing the foreword to this book. Those who would wish to share his stimulating experiences from walking the length of Great Britain and through countries of Europe will do so by reading his books

Journey Through Britain
and
Journey Through Europe (publ. Constable)

Foreword

There was a time and not so long ago when everybody walked, purposively. Poets such as Wordsworth, Tennyson and Coleridge composed some of their finest lines, alone, away from the madding crowd. Country parsons set up sermon-walks in the distant corners of their gardens. Walking for the thoughtful was recognized for what it is, an intimate association with the earth, an opportunity to refresh and reintegrate ourselves in the ever changing company of the landscape and the sky. For others it was the normal way of getting from one place to another. But when the car became commonplace and motoring an obsession, walking progressively declined. At least it did until a few years ago when the motorways began to dull the senses even of those who drive from their front doors to the nearest pillar box. Nowadays, I am hopeful that the pendulum is swinging back to a very old way of life.

As a Yorkshireman with a cottage in the very heart of the North Riding I can think of no place with more associations with walkers. It was from the great prayer houses of Jarrow, Jervaulx and Lindisfarne that the Venerable Bede, Alcuin and St. Cuthbert sent their emissaries, those men called the Athletes of God, south across the moors on the first limb-stretching leg of their transalpine walks to Lombardy and Rome. As I stand on the pannier trods of Westerdale I think of Celts carrying gold from Ireland to Gaul. But this is long-distance stuff.

I am passionately addicted to it myself, but never a day passes in my little retreat from the discontents of a big city without at least a modest stroll around the old iron workers' tracks of Rosedale, north to Danby, south on to Spaunton Moor, east to Cropton and Saltergate and west to Rudland Rigg. It is for happy indolents that Geoffrey White has bound together a network of wonderful trails of this kind. And I wish him as I wish you all many, many pleasurable years in which to enjoy our uncommon passion.

JOHN HILLABY

Introduction

THERE are several excellent comprehensive guides to the North York Moors, of value to the tourist, geologist, naturalist, antiquarian and specialist in many fields. Books have been written describing cross-moorland walks and holidays in selected areas. In this book, the first of two which together will take the motorist into the best parts of the National Park, I have set out to do something different: it is for those who want to do rather more than park the car and take a gentle stroll.

But just in case the reader is unfamiliar with the Moors and wishes to make a preliminary survey, I recommend the following parking places (not in order of merit) from which a stroll will be rewarding:

1 The car park below the White Horse, Kilburn.
2 Sutton Bank top.
3 Kepwick Bank top.
4 Sheepwash in Scarth Nick, between Osmotherley and Swainby.
5 Carlton Bank top, south-east of Carlton-in-Cleveland.
6 Clay Bank top car park, south-east of Great Broughton.
7 Chop Gate car park in Bilsdale.
8 Ellers Wood car park, north-west of Hawnby.
9 Newgate Bank, 5 miles north of Helmsley on the Stokesley road.
10 Cowhouse Bank, beyond Carlton, north-east of Helmsley.
11 Ousegill Bridge, between Fadmoor and Bransdale.
12 Blakey Ridge, north of Hutton-le-Hole.

The list is by no means exhaustive but if a sample is taken and the appetite whetted, the motorist may be tempted to explore the hills and dales more closely and I hope this book will be of help.

All the walks are *circular* and there is a map for each walk, intended to be self-explanatory, but the reader is strongly recommended to obtain a copy of the Ordnance Survey Tourist Map of the North York Moors, 1 : 50,000 or 1 inch to the mile, which will add enormously to the pleasure and interest of the excursion.

The area can be wild and exciting, attracting long distance walkers, the most noteworthy journey being the Lyke Wake Walk—40 miles from east to west on stretches of moor away from all human habitation. The Cleveland Way, sponsored by the Countryside Commission and opened in 1969, starts in Helmsley and goes three-quarters of the way round the perimeter of the Park, finishing down the coast at Filey. From the White Horse at Kilburn to Roseberry Topping in the north there is the White Rose Walk, 40 miles long or 34 miles if a shorter route is taken. Circular routes have been devised including the Rosedale Circuit, 37 miles; and a competitive 53 mile marathon, the Crosses Walk, linking many of the isolated crosses on the wild tops. Most of the country encountered on these long walks can be reached by the casual walker from his car.

If the gentler scene be preferred, there are peaceful dales, streams, woodlands and pastures to explore, villages to pass through, built of mellow sandstone and tiles, blending perfectly into the scene. The air is like wine and here one must feel that God's in His Heaven, All's right with the world. The moors can be subject to the sudden onset of mists but, compared to most northern uplands, the climate is comparatively dry.

I have tried to vary the walks as between hills and valleys and it may interest the reader to know my favourites:

Moorland Walks: Nos. 16 and 17
Mixed Uplands and Lowlands: Nos. 9 and 27
Wooded Valleys: Nos. 2 and 23
Special at Daffodil Time: No. 25

Changes of circumstances, such as the recognition of more rights of way, could easily alter the order of my choice.

NATIONAL PARK GUIDE No. 4 Published by H.M. Stationery Office at 35p.

This book is of great assistance and interest not only to those who wish to pursue hobbies in the National Park but also to the walker who needs no further hobby to enhance his enjoyment. On the subject of access to land, I should like to quote from the Guide: "Being easily accessible by road the National Park affords all-the-year-round exploration, but it is the walker or horseman who may best enjoy the intimacy of the Park for he may wander almost where he will. Access is remarkably free but, if in doubt, a polite enquiry will usually open all gates." In spite of these encouraging words, Walks for Motorists has been written using only definitive rights of way or the walks allowed by the Forestry Commission where entry is allowed to walkers but not to motorists.

The concession to walkers, who presumably do not present so great a fire hazard as motorists, does much to compensate for the damage to the scene caused in the early days of the Commission by the unimaginative planting of rank upon rank of dark pine trees. My plea now to the Forestry Commission is to leave many areas unplanted, especially below the edges of hillsides, so as to provide unrestricted views.

"WALKING OVER THE MOORS"

This leaflet issued by the National Park Planning Authority gives some useful advice to all who walk for pleasure across open moorland. If your activities take you beyond the limits of the suggested walks in this book, you are strongly recommended to obtain a copy of the leaflet and to follow its advice on the following subjects: What clothing and equipment do I need? How many in a party and how far? Long Distance Walking; Coastal Walks; What can I do in an emergency? If the weather turns bad; Before you go leave information with someone at home about your intended route and time of return.

The walker on short routes would also do well to take the tips given in the leaflet; the following advice applies to everybody and I quote verbatim:

Unexploded shells can still be found on the moors. For your own safety they must be left absolutely undisturbed. Please note the exact location, mark the spot with a few large stones and report the details to a local police station.

Adder Bite. The moors are the home of the adder, the only poisonous snake in Britain. It is vital to keep the patient at rest and reassure them they will not die. A firm bandage (not too tight) may be applied on the heart side of the bite. Loosen this bandage for one minute every thirty minutes. Telephone the police; rescue will be arranged and the patient will be taken for hospital treatment.

Search and Rescue. Thanks to the Police and the North York Moors Rescue Teams, your personal safety on the moor is highly valued. Over the years, their services have been a welcome relief to those walkers who have been stranded on the moors.

Much more information is given but in the meantime for the casual walker I would recommend the wearing of strong footwear (however short the journey I always prefer walking boots for the support they give to the ankles and for the grip on the ground); thick socks; waterproof, preferably an anorak or cagoule; and warm clothing. Carry, in addition to this guide, a 1 inch or 1 : 50,000 O.S. map and compass, chiefly for interest but you may get lost; rucksack; some food, even if it is your intention to return for a meal; and a first aid kit.

THE COUNTRY CODE

Guard against fire risks
Fasten all gates
Keep dogs under proper control
Keep to paths across farm land
Avoid damaging fences, hedges and walls
Leave no litter
Safeguard water supplies
Protect wild life, wild plants and trees
Go carefully on country roads
Respect the life of the countryside.

Walk 1 Helmsley and Whinny Bank Wood -4 miles (6·5 km)

(Including a part of the Cleveland Way)

NOT everybody wants to walk the whole of the way of a long-distance footpath but most people who like a walk show an interest in its direction and are pleased to travel on parts of it. Helmsley is not in Cleveland but the walk is well named, the path leading to the north-west parts of the North York Moors, the Cleveland Hills, cliff lands and the most dramatic area of the National Park.

From Helmsley the Cleveland Way goes westward to the White Horse at Kilburn, north by cliffs and along the famous Drove Road to the Clevelands, east to the coast and south along the coastal path to Filey, 100 miles in all. Today we shall walk along the first two miles of it! And as if to add insult to injury, the return route could follow the same track—not a very good start for a book which sets out to provide circular walks, but the aspect on the return is quite different and an alternative route is offered for those who obtain permission from the Estate Office in Helmsley to pass through Duncombe Park.

Helmsley is a lovely little Ryedale market town and an ideal holiday centre for the moors, having plenty of hotel and private accommodation and a Youth Hostel. Make your way through the market place, past the parish church and opposite the Feversham Arms there is an opening between houses sign-posted "Footpath to Rievaulx". Take this narrow lane leading over stiles through three fields. At the fourth stile there is another finger post showing a sharp turn to the left. Do not go over the stile but keep to the hedge side until, on reaching a wall above the woods, you turn right and, after passing through two gates (or over adjoining ladder-stiles) go through a gate in the wall you have been keeping on your left. Cross a small ravine into a beech wood. Keep now to the left of the wall and on emerging from the wood take a careful note of your surroundings so that if you are to return the same way you will note where you are to leave the main track and go along the side of the wall.

So, continuing on the outward journey and coming out of the wood on to a main track, a lodge (Griff Lodge) can be seen in front of you. Pass in front of it and through a gate on to the track above Whinny Bank Wood. Go forward until you reach a gap in the trees. The views of Ryedale from here are magnificent; tree-clad

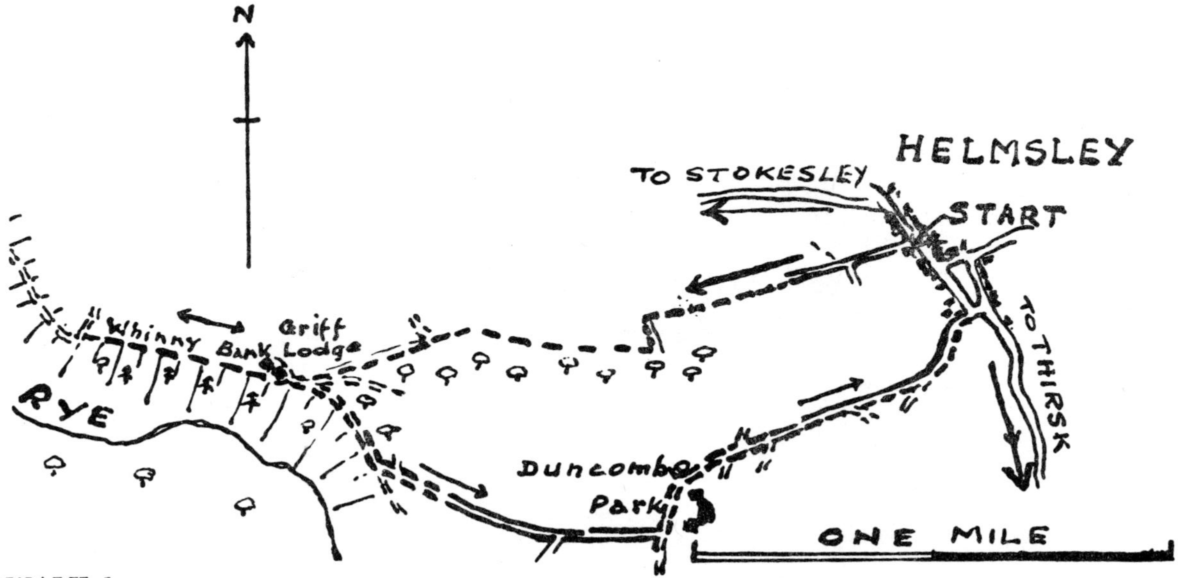
HELMSLEY
TO STOKESLEY
START
TO THIRSK
N
Whinny Bank
Griff Lodge
RYE
Duncombe Park
ONE MILE

WALK 1

steep sides to the valleys, pasture land below, and moorland beyond. This view is the main object of the day and it is a matter of preference whether to go on and how far. The river below is the Rye which has come into this valley a mile higher up, from the north. The valley straight ahead is the one along which the Cleveland Way goes—Nettledale.

Retrace your steps to Griff Lodge. If you have not obtained permission to walk through the park, leave the main track at the point where you emerged from the beech wood and join the old path leading to the wall, which now keep on your left. Cross the ravine again and go through the gate on the other side. Turn right and keep to the side of the wood until the path naturally takes you to the left alongside the hedge to the stile. Turn right, go over it and go straight on along the clear track with stiles back to Helmsley and the car.

Those able to pass through Duncombe Park will continue from Griff Lodge through the beech wood on the main track which will be seen to be concreted and which passes several concrete hard standings—evidence of armoured occupation during the Second World War. After about a quarter of a mile, where the track diverges, bear left and leave the wood on a farm track which crosses the park towards the big house, which is now a girls' school but is the former seat of the Earls of Feversham. The road bears to the left, crossing in front of the school and then to the right, crosses a cattle grid and continues downhill to the main gates, before which there are good views on the left to Helmsley Castle—also worth a visit. Turn left towards the market place after leaving Duncombe Park.

Walk 2 Rievaulx, Nettledale, Caydale, and Ryedale-7 miles (11 km)

NO visitor to the National Park should fail to visit Rievaulx Abbey, the first big Cistercian church to be built in England, begun in 1131 and almost completed by 1175. The setting in the Rye valley is perfect: the surrounding hills and trees add beauty to the scene and the little village of Rievaulx is itself worth a visit. Rievaulx Terrace, above the Abbey, should not be missed, with its half a mile of lawn, two classical temples and the best views of the Abbey.

Our walk will include the early stages of the Cleveland Way and some very fine valley and woodland scenery. We start from the vicinity of the Abbey car park (which is for the use of visitors to the Abbey only). There will probably be room to park beside the river to the south of the Abbey. You could, however, motor on to the gate at the bend of the road to Scawton (see below). If you do this you could consider an alternative return from Bow Bridge round Ashberry Hill. The going is good, especially if one adds a mile to the distance by going up Blind Side and Tanker Dale instead of up through the woods and fields from Nettledale to Old Byland on an ancient bridleway which is not so much used nowadays. The village of Old Byland is of interest inasmuch as it is where the monks from Furness Abbey first settled before going to Byland Abbey, four miles away.

Rievaulx (sometimes pronounced Rivis locally) is signposted a little over two miles out of Helmsley on the Stokesley road. Motor downhill, through the village, past the Abbey entrance which is on the left. Leaving the car, continue south on foot on the road which is soon joined by the River Rye, sometimes babbling over stones, sometimes in peaceful pools. On reaching the bridge (Rievaulx Bridge) turn right and pause to admire the tranquillity of the scene here and at Ashberry Farm. The next section of the walk forms part of the Cleveland Way. Continue west along the road until it bends towards Scawton, at which point take the gate on the right, go along the track above the stream and where that track in turn goes off to the left leave it and cross a stout sleeper bridge over the clear limestone stream to a wicket gate and a path through a thicket. Take only fifteen paces on this path and leaving the Cleveland Way, turn to the right on to a less-clear path which takes you to a stile into the water meadow, which cross near to the stream to another stile and a moss-covered plank over the beck. Go over it gingerly and take the path to the left sloping up the hill through the woods.

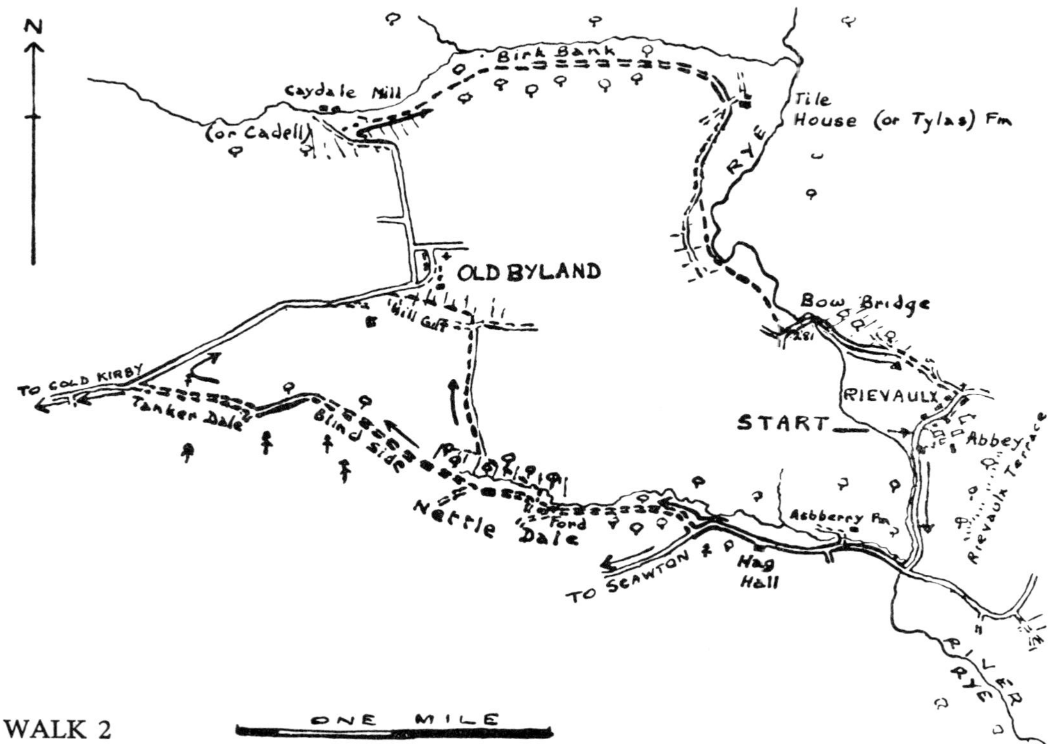
N
Birk Bank
Caydale Mill
(or Cadell)
Tile
House (or Tylas) Fm
RYE
OLD BYLAND
Mill Gill
Bow Bridge
281
RIEVAULX
START
Abbey
Rievaulx Terrace
TO COLD KIRBY
Tanker Dale
Blind Side
Nettle Dale
Ford
Abberry Fm
TO SEAWTON
Hag
Hall
RIVER
RYE
ONE MILE

WALK 2

Soon the track becomes less clear but keep in the same general direction and it quickly improves right away to the top where it passes through a gate into a ploughed field. Turn north along the hedge side. Leaving the field through a gate, make for another gate at the other side of a narrow pasture. Go through it and turn left along the side of the ravine and the path will slope down to the valley bottom and continue upwards to a gate on to the road just outside the village of Old Byland (close to the County Council mill-wheel village sign). A simpler route (but adding a little more than a mile to the journey) would be, instead of turning right after fifteen paces, continue up Nettledale, do not turn left at the "Moors Path" sign at three beech trees, but go straight ahead up Blind Side along the forest road until reaching the tarred road on which turn to the right to Old Byland.

Take the road northwards from Old Byland for Caydale Mill (Cadell Mill on some maps) and at the turning to the left at the top of the hill stop to admire the valley view. Go down the road almost to the bottom of the hill and through a gate on the right to join a track downstream through the woods at Birk Bank. Continue south when joining the metalled road above Tylas Farm for half a mile, then take to the path by the River Rye as far as the bridge at height 281 (Bow Bridge) and then along the road to Rievaulx.

ASHBERRY FARM

Walk 3 Round Easterside Hill-4½ miles (7 km)

MOTORING north on the Helmsley to Stokesley road, it is worth pausing at the car park and viewpoint at the top of Newgate Bank (not named on the tourist map but shown as being 803 feet above sea level) for a magnificennt view of Bilsdale to the north and the tabular hills above Hawnby to the north-west. The nearer one is Easterside Hill, today's objective, and the view from the top of it must be one of the best in the district. It does not, however, carry a right of way over the summit so let us walk round it instead of over it for a good walk by a farm track, a moorland way through heather and a minor road, all with fine views.

Motor north for another mile and take the first turn left, passing over the bridge (River Seph) at Laskill as far as the hairpin bend to the north of the bridge. Take the minor road straight on (sign-posted "No through road") and park 70 yards further on where there is room at another hairpin bend for more than a dozen cars.

Walk along this road, continuing in a northerly direction up Bilsdale. Across the valley is Roppa Plantation on the northern escarpment of Helmsley Moor and the trees in the valley bottom hide the River Seph, the principal stream in Bilsdale. After passing two farm houses the road turns uphill and before the top is reached there is a milk churn platform on the right. Take the track to the left just beyond, first between hedges, then through a field to a farm, Ewe Cote. There are animals about and gates to close. At the far end of the farm yard bear right and make for the gate leading to a green lane between walls, going uphill, soon leading to another gate to open fields. The track can be seen going upwards through the right-hand field ahead.

Once through a gate leading on to open moor, continue straight forward on the track which goes into a gulley and after less than a hundred yards the gulley divides into two. Walk between the two gulleys and join a cart track which can just be seen in the heather. If you pause here to admire the scene you will notice that Easterside on your left has a very steep northern aspect; immediately in front of you is Hawnby Hall, an isolated tabular similar in many ways to Easterside; to the right in the north can be seen, in reasonably good weather, the television mast on Bilsdale West Moor. There is heather all round which is at its best in late August or early September which, unfortunately for the rambler, coincides with the shooting season. To miss the shoot at this time of the year it is as well to avoid walking over this right of way on Saturdays.

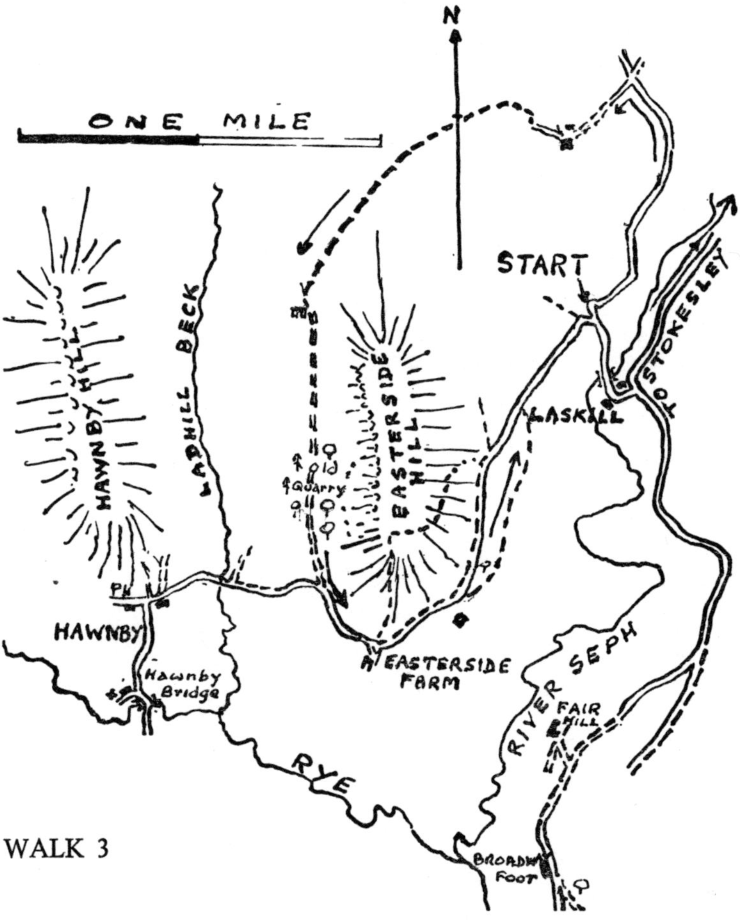

WALK 3

Ahead is a wall and the track makes a bee-line for a gap in it. Lovely Ryedale is below, well wooded, and with the tabular Arden Great Moor as a back cloth. Through the wall the track becomes less discernible but it makes for the upper side of a wire fence. Keep to the left of the fence until within about 300 yards of the farm, High Banniscue, where go through a gate and make for the farm, passing over a stile. Keep above the farm and join the farm road which continues at the same level on the hillside. When the road reaches conifers look across to the right front for a glimpse of the village of Hawnby nestling among the hills. Keep on the stone road and when the junction is reached, turn left on the tarmac road. Up on Easterside to the left can be seen some clear tracks but our route continues on the tarred road for about half a mile during which pass a farm on the right, Easterside Farm, and another one at a milk churn table below on the right. A hundred yards beyond this table go through a gate on the right and take the green track, roughly parallel to the road, through bracken and scattered trees. Then for about a quarter of a mile keep above the level of a hedge, over a stile and continue for about half the length of the next field where the track goes through the hedge and makes for the disused cottage ahead. Skirt below this, pass a broken down outbuilding and join a track leading to a stile back to the road. Continue on the road downhill to the sharp bend, turn left at the sign "No through road" and back to the car 70 yards further on.

EASTERSIDE AND HAWNBY HILL

Walk 4 Thorodale-7 miles (11km)

THE lovely little village of Hawnby, situated on a hillside and surrounded by tabular hills of notable shape, can easily be reached by car from Helmsley by taking the Stokesley road and turning left soon after the third milestone. It can also be reached from Thirsk via Boltby and Sneck Yate Bank or from Osmotherley on the narrow road via Snilesworth, all three routes presenting most beautiful scenery.

The walk passes through wooded country and into the secluded bracken-covered valley of Thorodale, out on the famous Drove Road for a glimpse of the Vale of Mowbray and, with luck, of the Pennines beyond, and back along a road unsuitable for motors, giving views of the lake in the valley below.

Take the Kepwick road out of Hawnby, suitable for motors in its early stages but not later on, and park the car by the roadside on the grass verge near New Hall, about a mile out of the village. It would not be feasible to accommodate a large number of cars here. They could be left in Hawnby and this would add two more miles to the total journey. Probably a better place for parking beside this same road is above Arden Hall, further on. A short cut could then be made past the Hall itself, where there is a right-of-way. This also avoids the field which may be occupied by a bull, as described below.

Walking from New Hall take the cart track between the buildings on the right hand side of the road leading downhill between bushes. To the right is an impressive view of Hawnby Hill Crag. At the bottom of the track cross a sleeper bridge over a clear stream and continue forward with the woodland on your left. Emerging from the woods into a field keep on the right hand side of the field until a cart track is reached on which turn left, pass through a farm yard and turn left again. This is on a farm road, over a cattle grid adjoining which is a gate bearing the sign "Beware of the Bull". The track across the field ahead is a right of way; on several visits to the area the writer has not seen the bull and fortunately there are only 200 yards to traverse to a triangular clump of trees before leaving the field through a gate on the right. For the next two miles the walk goes through Thorodale in which Arden Hall is well situated. The track through the next field takes us up to the cart track leading down to Arden Hall on the left, but continue forward on the obvious track, keeping the wood on our left. Ignore tracks leading down through the wood and up the hillside. Looking down through the trees you might catch a glimpse of the shimmering waters of the lake but there will be no general view of its outline until the return journey is made.

As the path emerges towards the open moor it tends to go downwards to the head of the valley. At this point go through a gate on the right and continue forward on a forestry road until a hairpin bend is reached at the stream. Just before the loop go forward on a slight path on the right and keep to the stream, which is narrow, crossing and re-crossing until it is reduced to four streamlets. It is worth a pause here to appreciate the peace of the dale with its tongues and nicks and slopes of bracken. An isolated hawthorn tree indicates the point of ascent from the valley, and a hard look will reveal the position of the track sloping upwards from left to right. Just beyond the hawthorn it is somewhat marshy but soon the only obstacle to upward progress should be, in high summer, the shoulder-high bracken. At the top it is worth looking back.

There is a wall at the top. Go up to it and continue in a westerly direction, keeping the wall on your left. Another stone wall appears in front of you, and you should see a gate. Make for it and beyond it pass some old workings to the ruins of Lime Kiln House on the Drove Road. Years ago Lime Kiln was a public house serving chiefly the drovers who used this ancient way to bring their cattle from Scotland to the markets of the south, chiefly York and Malton. The herds would be driven through Yarm and on to the high ground of the North York Moors at Scarth Nick near Swainby, over Black Hambleton and south past where we are now standing to the Hambleton Hotel and beyond. Nowadays the road is used a great deal by walkers and it has been incorporated into the Cleveland Way and the White Rose Walk.

On a clear day the view from here is superb. It is pretty below around the villages of Kepwick and the Siltons, Nether and Over, and the extensive views over the Vale of Mowbray include Wensleydale, with Penhill on its southern edge and, south of that, Great Whernside above the general line of the Pennines.

We shall walk south on the Drove Road today but only for less than half a mile as far as the cross track where the road from Kepwick appears through a gate in the wall. This again is the road marked as unsuitable for motors (but a fair number venture up the steep bank from Kepwick) and at this point turn left on the track which leads back to Hawnby. It goes through open moor to start with and after a gate, through fields which overlook Thorodale, now on the left, and it is from here that the lake in its forest setting can best be seen. The road slopes steeply down the side of the valley and through the extensive woods. The surface of the road is rough until it enters the region of Arden Hall when it becomes a motor road but the walker is unlikely to be disturbed by many vehicles. The turning for Arden Hall is to the left but keep straight on for another mile and you will reach the car.

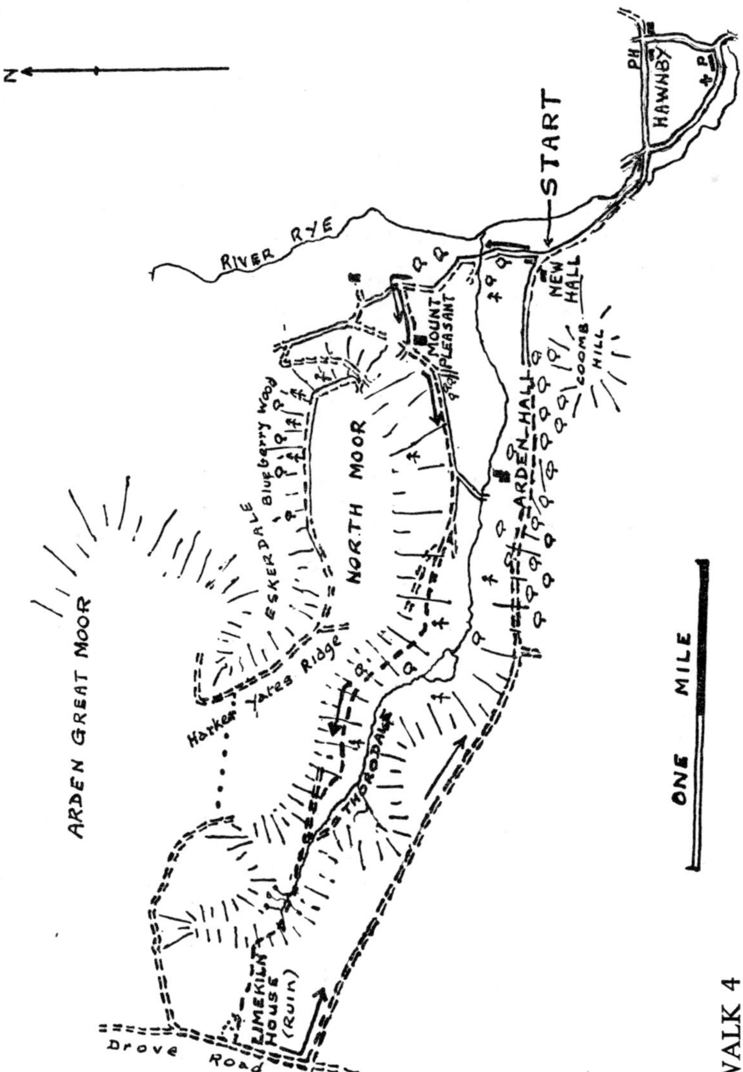

WALK 4

Walk 5 Alongside Hawnby Hill and around Coomb Hill-5 miles (8 km)

IT is unfortunate that because there is no right of way over the top of the central feature in the Hawnby area the reader cannot be guided along this fine hog's back which provides an exhilarating mile of ridge walking. But instead, let us take tracks as of right leading to some lovely places and across the River Rye to fine woodlands.

Motoring north on the Osmotherley road from Hawnby there are some good picnic places on the side of Hawnby Hill well and truly used by amblers and scramblers. A quarter of a mile further north park the car near the junction of several tracks, known as Moor Gate.

Twenty yards uphill from the foundations of an old wall take a green double track in the heather. The track skirts to the right of Hawnby Hill which looks very impressive from here. With views of Upper Ryedale on the right, follow the track as far as a wire fence where it becomes more pronounced: keep the fence on your right and pass through a gateway into a fenced lane leading to a sheep-cropped track between clumps of bracken on the hillside above Hill End House. Deciduous trees are on the left and there are good views up Thorodale on the right with Coomb Hill, tree covered, to the right front.

Before going out of sight of Hill End House go through a gate after which there are oak trees on the left and a fence on the right. Emerging from the trees, through a gate, turn downhill along a slight slope at the foot of which another track is joined and ahead can be seen the first of the farms of Hawnby village. Make for it and unless refreshment is required at the Hawnby Hotel, turn right on the tarmac road downhill, beyond the cross-roads where there is a notice saying "Unsuitable for motors 1½ miles ahead"; cross the bridge over the River Rye and turn left immediately beyond the bridge wall; climb a stile and follow a cart track for 50 yards by the side of the river; turn uphill to the right towards a tree and then a telepgraph pole; follow a green track through the corner of the wood ahead; pass through a gate into a clearing and continue on the track through the bracken. A grass-cum-dirt track leads to a gate near the top of the valley after which it circles round the wood to the right. North Moor, now exposed because of tree felling, is in view to the front. Go through a gate and bear round to the right again to another gate leading to a track through the woods. It is downhill now all the way to where the track almost reaches a tarmac road. Cross six feet or

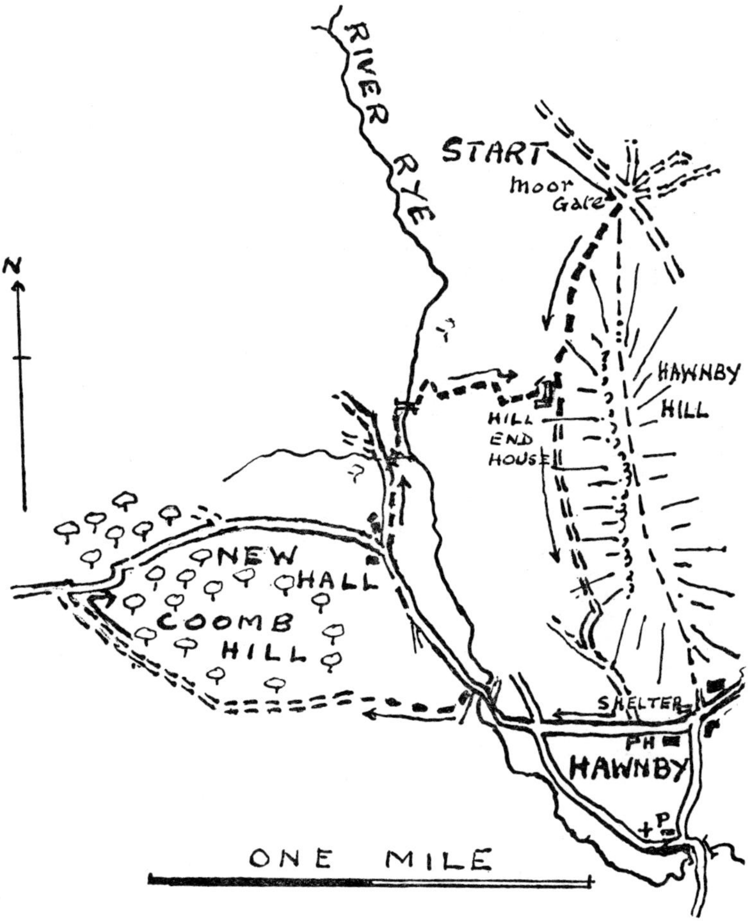

WALK 5

so to it and turn to the right, going downhill. (This is the road which was marked as being unsuitable for motors.)

Ahead can be seen the cliffs of Hawnby Hill, when a clearing is reached, and the farm below the cliffs is Hill End House which will be rejoined later on. When the first buildings by the roadside are arrived at, turn down left on the green lane immediately before reaching the left-hand-side buildings; pass a little cottage on the left and take the track ahead between bushes (there is no gateway to pass through). In woods again keep to the track leading down to a clear stream over which there is a strong plank bridge but do not go over it; instead go through the gateway on the right leading to a path across the corner of the field and cross a well-constructed wooden bridge. Walk down the left bank of the stream and bear left at the edge of the wood. Through the woods and below on the right is the young River Rye which cross about 200 yards ahead on a metal bridge. Turn to the left on the other side where the direction of the path is clear but is little used. It goes slightly uphill for about 200 yards, bears right for about 50 yards and then bears left again directly uphill, all the time in woods, leading to a gate in the corner of a field. Go through the gate and turn right keeping to the side of the wood which is soon left behind. Continue alongside the hedge to a gate near the top right-hand corner of the field; go through it and cut across the corner of the adjoining field to another gate 60 yards away. Hill End House is now one field away, uphill. Make for the gate on the right of the house which gives access to the track used earlier. Continue uphill on this track towards the gate at the top at which keep on the track which bears to the right, keeping to the right-hand side of the fence.

The direction of travel is now towards the television mast (Bilsdale) but a nearer landmark is a group of three windswept trees to the left front. Before reaching the level of the trees the car should be in sight.

Walk 6 Cow Ridge, Head House and Arnsgill Ridge-6 miles (9·5 km)

THIS is a walk on good tracks through lovely heather country, up one side of the valley of Arns Gill and down the other. It is in typical Upper Ryedale country and the ridges are respectively arms of Bilsdale West Moor and Snilesworth Moor. Because the plan of the walk is so simple and the going so good there is a great opportunity here to step out at a reasonable pace, take in great gulps of pure air, and admire the stretches of moorland, ridge upon ridge.

On the Hawnby-Osmotherley road two miles north-west of Moor Gate, which was the start point of Walk No. 5, there is a turning northwards off the road, to Scotland Farm. Going towards Osmotherly from Hawnby by car, first pass Moor Gate, which is at the foot of Hawnby Hill; a mile further on there is a fine viewpoint at Ellers Wood which is worth a stop; continuing in the same direction the road goes downhill through woods, over Blow Gill—a pretty spot where there is a footbridge—and rises from it for half a mile and soon after taking a sharp left turn, the road to Scotland Farm is on the right. Take it for a few hundred yards and where it bends down to the farm, park the car near a forestry gate instead of taking the bend. The area may be recognised as forestry land at a post marked R.P.6 but at the time of writing no visible planting had been done.

Approaching the start point from the direction of Osmotherley, look out for the bridge over the infant River Rye where there is a green sward often used as a picnic place for car parties or a meeting place for car supporters of walkers on the White Rose Walk. The turn towards Scotland Farm is a mile further on—the first on the left.

Walkers go through the gate and on to the clear track which leads past a succession of tumuli on the left and climbs steadily upwards on Cow Ridge. Soon at the head of the valley on the left, Arns Gill, will be seen Head House but walk for at least a mile before taking a track to the left off the main one which goes straight on. Always Head House is in sight and it is soon reached after the path crosses the stream. The building is a disused farm house but is kept in good repair and commands a very fine view down the valley. Cross in front of the house and continue crossing to the other side of the valley to join another good track which, on turning left, brings you to the return journey on Arnsgill Ridge.

At this point there may be some who would like to extend the walk by a couple of miles by turning right instead of left, to take you up to a tumulus, Green Howe, a mile away, from which there are good views of Scugdale and Raisdale; then back along the same track to Head House.

The going down the Arnsgill Ridge is straightforward for nearly two miles. Pass over a cattle grid down to Hill End Farm which is skirted by taking a right turn through the farm gate on to the farm road which turns immediately left and leads through a field to a gate where it joins a public road on which turn left. You will not meet much traffic here—it is the link with the world for Rye Farm. Cross the River Rye by a foot bridge at a water splash and continue to Low Cote Farm where you join the Osmotherley-Hawnby road, narrow but much used on summer Sundays. Continue downhill past the picnic place, over the bridge, and a mile further on is the turning for the car. Single file walking on the right of the road is strongly recomended.

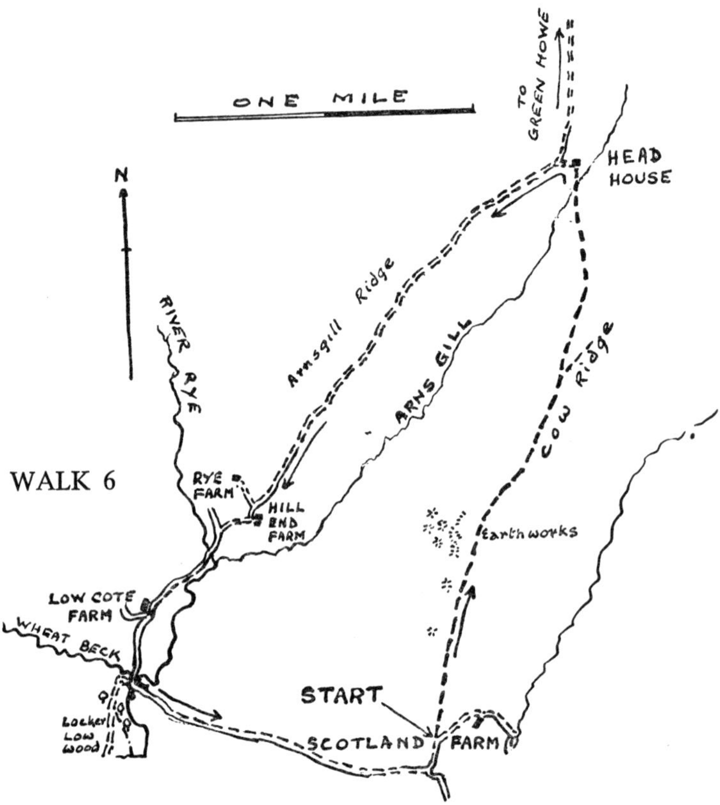

WALK 6

Walk 7 Wass, Observatory, Oldstead and Byland Abbey-5 miles (8 km)

SPRINGTIME, probably late May, is an ideal season in which to make this short expedition: the countryside is at its loveliest; the pretty villages are in their setting of apple blossom amid the woods and hills and the woods are filled with the perfume of bluebells. An opportunity may be taken to visit Byland Abbey (established 1177), a fine ruin in a wide valley and there are good views over the Vale of York from the observatory above Snever Wood.

From the crossroads at Wass, on the Thirsk-Helmsley low road (a 'bus route), take the road to the north-west indicated "No road for Motors" passing some attractive houses and gardens with a little stream by the side of the road. Go over a cattle grid, past a pond and where the metalled road bears to the right and there is a gate into the woods on the left, go straight on and over a kind of stile into a field at the woodside. When the fence on the left curves to the right in front and becomes a wall make your way uphill to a middle height, go through a gateway and take the right-hand, upper ride through the forest. Keep to the right at all forks until a wall is reached at the top of the wood. Remain within the forest boundary, with the wall on your right and at the third ride on the left, the square tower of the observatory will be seen. Go to it. A plaque on one of the walls tells us it was erected in the first year of the reign of Queen Victoria.

Access to the footpath leading down to Oldstead is obtained through a gate. The path is rough but distinct and it descends quickly to a rough clay forest ride. Turn right and look out for views previously obscured by trees. Two and a half miles to the south is the lake in the grounds of Newburgh Priory. Oldstead comes into sight below; over to the right is Cockerdale; to the in 1322 Robert Bruce beat Edward II in the Battle of Byland. NNW across the valley, now well wooded, is Scotch Corner where A little further to the west the rear of the White Horse can be seen and the top of Hood Hill. The well-wooded valley into which we are descending is one cut by glacial meltwaters.

The clay track goes down to a metalled forest road; turn right on it; after 400 yards turn left at a T junction; pass through a gateway on to a farm road and turn left. At a gate marked "Cockerdale" turn again left and still once more left at the junction to pass through Oldstead built in the distinctive style of the district. At the "Black Swan" take the Byland Abbey road and just beyond the millstone sign marked "Oldstead" turn to the right at the farm gate with the sign "Oldstead Grange—Bed and Breakfast".

Pass through the farm yard and gateway at the other side and on a cart track to the bottom of the next field where there is a gate. Go through it and immediately turn off the cart track and make uphill on the left by the hedge side on a little-used old track to the buildings. Pass to the right of the house (Cams Head) where ahead will be seen the top ruins of Byland Abbey. Go towards it on the farm road which soon turns abruptly to the left, at which point go straight on and keep to the left of the stream for the right-of-way which has been ploughed up in places. But keep to the stream side until the track turns away by the side of a hedge in which there is a gate, beyond which the path crosses pasture to a gate leading to the yard of College Farm. On the public road turn right, pass under a stone arch and perhaps visit the Abbey or the Abbey Inn. It is not far back to Wass from here. It can be seen over to the left and is easily reached by road.

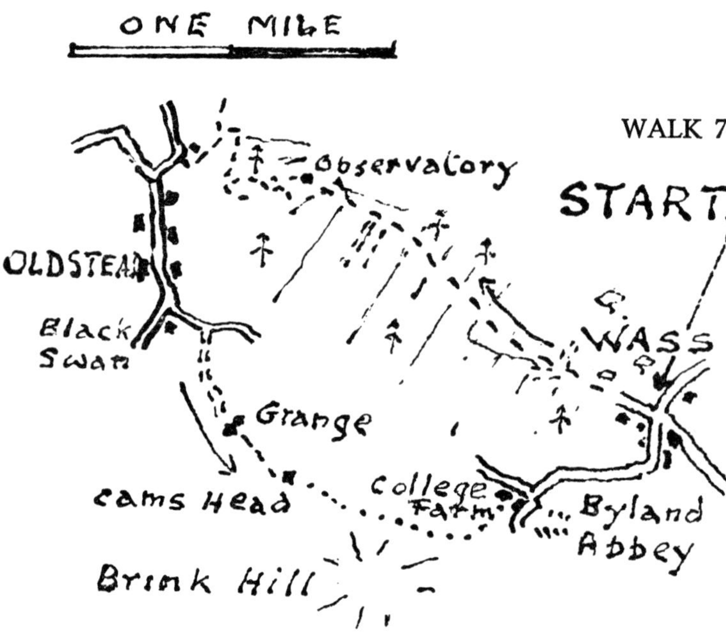

Walk 8 Oldstead, Scawton Moor and Flassen Dale-10½ miles (17 km)

A CONVENIENT start point is the north end of Oldstead village. The outward journey includes a walk over the Monks' Trod, which linked Rievaulx with Byland Abbey, across Scawton Moor which before the Second World War was a deer park on the Duncombe Park estate and was then a glorious mass of heather but has now been ploughed up. The return route includes parts of the Cleveland Way and back by Scots Corner (or Scotch Corner) where the Battle of Byland took place in 1322 when Robert Bruce defeated Edward II.

From Oldstead village can be seen, on the spur to the north, the attractive cottage designed for his own use by the architect, Charles Needham. Leave the car on the verge of the quiet road leading to it. Below the house is a gate marked Cockerdale Farms. Go through it and keep to the farm road. At the top of the first little hill go through the forestry gate on the right and turn left at the T junction above it. This forestry road leads upwards at a reasonable gradient and so long as the trees remain young, gives good views to the left of the pleasant valley of Cockerdale below. The road is made of rough shingle and continues towards the farm which can be seen on the hill top. Turn to the right when you meet a T junction at the head of the valley and make for the farm, Cam House, which is now unoccupied. Circle round the next farm, Cold Cam, and take the obvious farm road on to the main Thirsk-Helmsley road, on which turn to the right and walk for a mile, passing between coniferous woods at the end of which there is a bungalow on the left. The forest ride immediately opposite is the track from the Wass road. Just beyond the bungalow there are two sets of gates leading in and out of a small field and on to a clear track which passes two huge Dutch barns. This is the Monks' Trod, now ploughed up but well-defined and becoming sunken for a considerable distance. Pass through a wooden gate across the Trod or an iron gate by the side of it and look out for Rievaulx Terrace across Ryedale, a plain of green among the trees, below which the Abbey is situated. The Trod continues above a steep ravine and soon the Abbey itself can be seen.

A steep drop and a bend in the track soon brings you to the road near Ashberry Farm. Turn left along the road, part of the Cleveland Way.

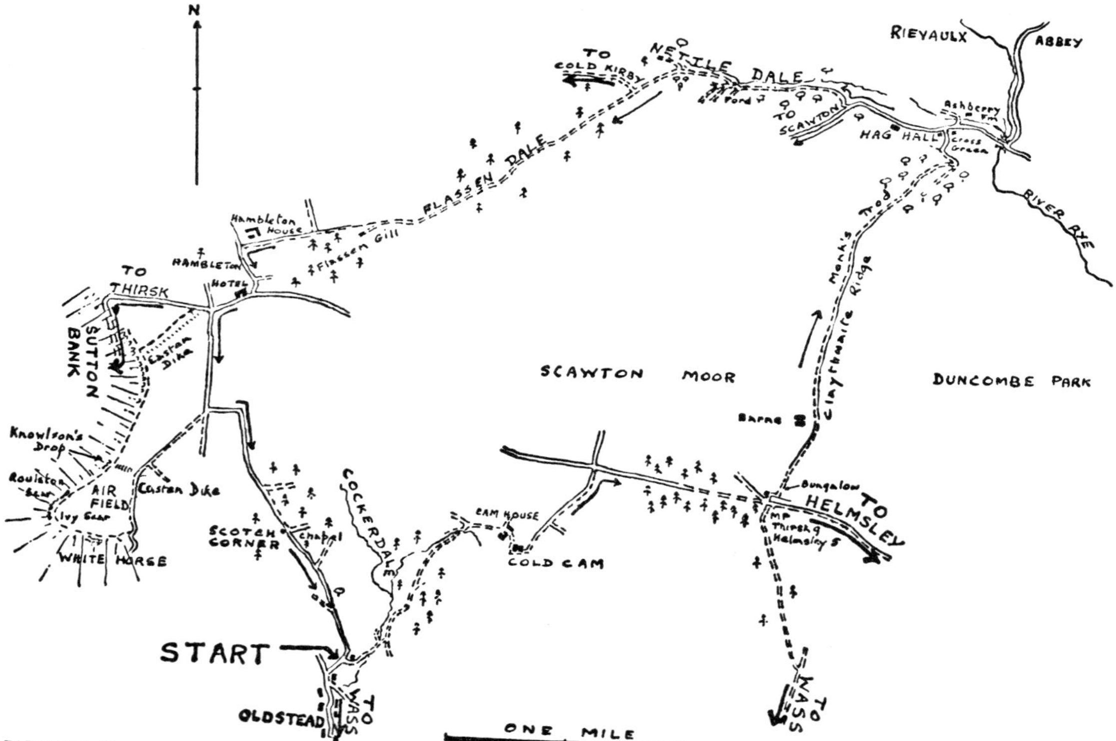
N
RIEYAULX
ABBEY
RIVER RYE
TO COLD KIRBY
NETTLE DALE
Ford
TO SCAWTON
Ashberry Fm
HAG HALL
Cross Green
FLASSEN DALE
Hambleton House
HAMBLETON HOTEL
Flassen Gill
TO THIRSK
SUTTON BANK
Casten Dike
Monk's Trod
Claythwaite Ridge
SCAWTON MOOR
DUNCOMBE PARK
Barns
Knowlson's Drop
Rouiston Scar
AIR FIELD
Ivy Scar
WHITE HORSE
SCOTCH CORNER
chapel
COCKERDALE
CAM HOUSE
COLD CAM
Bungalow
TO HELMSLEY
MP Thirsk 9 Helmsley 5
START
OLDSTEAD
TO WASS
ONE MILE
TO WASS

WALK 8

Opposite Hag Hall is a caravan site and Camping Club site; the road and stream come close together and 100 yards further on, at the bend of the road, there is a forestry gate and stile which leads you on to a drive through old deciduous trees, on many of which are nesting boxes, and continues by the side of the stream, which go over when you reach a plank bridge. Pass through a wicket gate and continue up-valley (Nettledale) until you reach the next valley junction where there should be a Moors Path sign indicating a left turn. This valley is Flassen Dale. Soon another Moors Path sign shows that the Cleveland Way turns off to the right but, instead of doing this today, continue up the valley on the Forestry Commission path for more than a mile when the path narrows and takes one upwards on the right, along the side of a small ravine to a well-established private spruce wood and keeps alongside it. Soon after leaving the valley there is a good stile on the right bringing in the long-distance route (marked with an Acorn sign) which has deviated to Cold Kirby. Keep straight on, climb over another stile and cross the field by the wall side leaving Hambleton House racing stables on the right. Cross another stile and turn to the left on the rough road. Then on the main road turn right and soon after passing the Hambleton Hotel turn left at the cross-roads. On the right is the site of the ancient Casten Dike, through coniferous trees.

Keep on this macadam road for half a mile and when it bends round to the right, turn left on the first of two green tracks which join the road. This lane soon bends round to the right; passes through forestry land, and past a moorland chapel, the site of the battle; as it goes downhill it becomes sunken but from time to time emerges to give views of Cockerdale from the other side and Oldstead below, nestling in the glorious wooded country between the Hambleton Hills and the low outliers to the south. Return to the car at the foot of the road.

Walk 9 White Horse, Grand Circle Route to Gormire and return along the top-6 miles (9·5 km)

THE beauty of this excursion is that it combines some lovely corners under the lee of the hills with the grandeur of the cliff walk back to the start point.

From the car park immediately below the Kilburn White Horse go through the gate at the north end, taking the upper ride in the forestry land. Where there are bifurcations keep under the cliff, ignoring an upward path, marked by a post with a red arrow, at Knowlson's Drop. From time to time there should be good glimpses of the Pennines and in suitable weather one can clearly see Penhill and Wensleydale but it is the local scene that is of particular interest today; Hood Hill with its two deciduous trees rising above the conifers makes a prominent landmark. Note the two indentations near the top. Are they intrenchments of an ancient stronghold?

Continuing north the cliffs on the right are impressive. Some say that a man on a white horse fell over the edge and the name of it, Knowlson's Drop, adds credence to the legend. Soon the grand circle engulfing Sutton Bank comes into view. There may be some who would prefer to call it the grand semi-circle but the sweeps to Hood Hill on the left and the hill south of Cleaves on the right (now being quarried away) almost enclose the area, suitably named Happy Valley. Down below can be seen a white house near which is a track leading northwards towards a farm; eventually the route leads past these points. Still on our good wide track, a flower lover's paradise, gliders may be well observed above, making use of the upward air currents. The green track emerges upon the hairpin bend of a rough gravel track. Take the one to the right which leads to the hairpin bend of the main road on Sutton Bank. Turn downhill. There is a ten-minute main road walk so take care. Less than a hundred yards on the left, unobserved by motorists, is a bronze age tomb of about 1,400 B.C.

At the foot of Sutton Bank turn right on the bridle road just before the white house and pass a pleasing water garden before the farm and the farm itself and when breasting the hill, the beautiful Lake Gormire lies below. The better way past the lake is by the path straight forward, to the right of it, through Garbutt Wood nature reserve, a lovely spot. Because of its sheltered position Gormire's waters seem seldom to be ruffled except by the occasional passing of moorhen or duck or the rising of the fish. At the north end of the lake keep to the clear path going forward which traverses some boggy land through woods and emerges at a neat house and garden shown on the 1-inch map as near spot height 470.

But before reaching the house, almost at the end of the wood, you pass two notice boards, one saying "Garbutt Wood" and the other "Yorkshire Naturalists Trust Ltd., Garbutt Wood Nature Reserve. Please do not pick flowers, uproot plants or molest wild life. Under no circumstances may fires be lit." Here take an acute right turn on the upward-sloping track. Seventy yards further up an arrow indicates "sloping path". Take it past the signs erected by the Trust indicating specimens to be observed and lettered from G to K. The path slopes upwards towards Whitestone Cliff ahead and then levels out well below the cliff until it joins a wider track.

The way ahead is now clear, rising steadily towards the crest of the hill. Pausing for breath and for another look at Gormire, one can see in the distance on a clear day Great Whernside beyond the lake and to the north, Wensleydale. Continue upwards until the track is reached along the cliff top and turn right. We are now in the middle of one of the finest parts of the Cleveland Way and the White Rose Walk—the escarpment of the Hambleton Hills. Below can be seen one of several "bays" beneath the cliffs. Beyond the bays are outliers of differing heights and all form lovely tracts of country.

The path now is on the top of high cliffs but for those without a head for heights there is no need to go near the edge. Gormire is below, described by many as a jewel in a perfect setting, and it really is a picture set amid the trees beneath the cliffs, named Whitestone Cliff or White Mare Crag. Of the many legends about these cliffs and this lake, reputed to be "bottomless", probably the best is one related by Bill Cowley in his book "The Cleveland Way". He tells of a witch, chased over the cliff by hounds, who fell into the lake and came up at a keld nine miles away.

Still keeping to the edge of the escarpment, the path passes a plantation, after which it comes out on to the main road at the top of Sutton Bank, which cross. On the other side is a direction indicator showing the distances to towns and features many miles away. The path continues along the top, past the end of the ancient Casten Dike; by the edge of the airfield of the Yorkshire Gliding Club; above the cliff known at Knowlson's Drop—but beware! Do not follow in Knowlson's footsteps—above two more cliffs known respectively as Roulston Scar and Ivy Scar and round the corner to the White Horse cut into the turf on Low Town Brow. The best known statistic is that 20 people can picnic on its eye. Other vital information is that, led by the Kilburn schoolmaster, Mr. John Hodgson, 30 people made it in 1857. The base is limestone, not chalk as with many White Horses cut into hillsides, and to be kept white it has to be covered with lime from time to time. It covers about 2 acres of ground; height 228 feet; length 314 feet. The lovely valley below leading to Oldstead, was cut by the meltwaters of the glacier, probably more than 10,000 years ago.

A flight of steps beyond the tail of the White Horse leads down to the car park below.

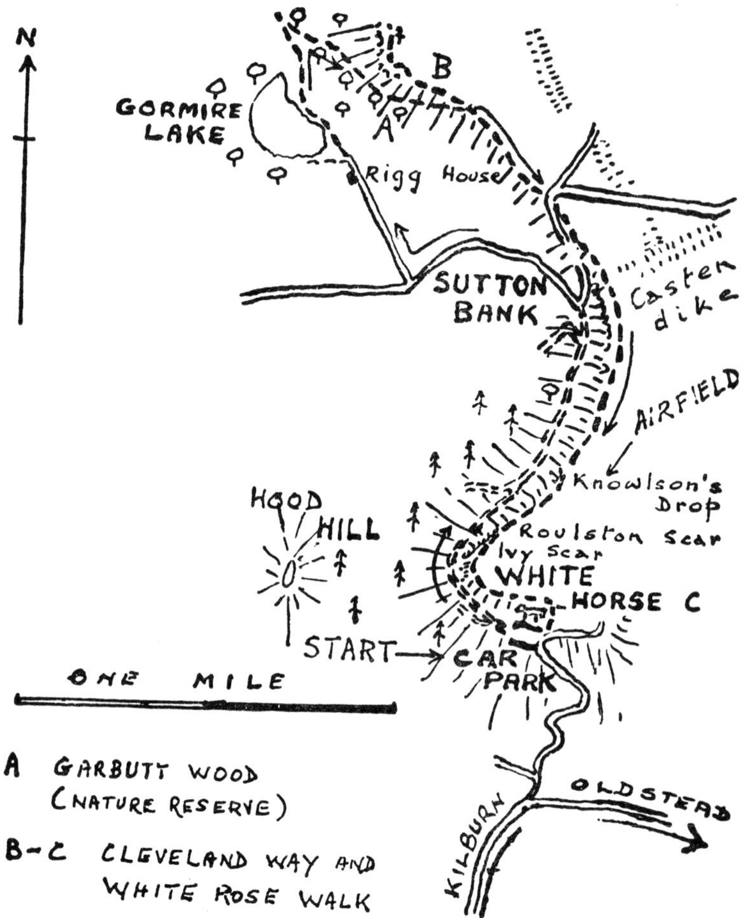

WALK 9

Walk 10 Boltby, Little Moor, Hill Fort and South Woods-5 miles (8 km)

IN this book there is quite a concentration of walks on or below the western cliffs of the National Park, simply because the pronounced features of crag, woodland, foot hills with valleys between, make the area one of delight and tranquillity. Moreover it is by no means overrun with people and it is ideal for those seeking peace and quietness.

Boltby is reached from Thirsk via Felixkirk, a pretty village on rising ground. The road between Felixkirk and Boltby is a pleasant one and it is worth stopping here and there for backward views across the plain. Boltby is a typical village on the fringe of the moors, built of local stone and tiles.

Park at the far end and take the by-road to the right just beyond the stream and make for the hills. Ahead on the skyline there are old quarry workings where there was once an aerial ropeway and to the right of the workings are some fine whitestone cliffs, Boltby Scar. Our first objective, the old hill fort, is just above and to the south of Boltby Scar. In the lane there is a ford and footbridge and then at the end of the lane enter the field ahead and make for the gate at the top right hand corner. There seem to be alternative routes on the other side through bracken and birches; take the one to the right leading to a gully, surely an ancient road, alongside which is a clear track, first on the right and then to the left of it at a point where there are some oak trees. Keep above the ditch until the track leads towards a heap of stones on Little Moor. Make for it and go through the gate and continue uphill, keeping the wall on your left. Another deep old bridleway is reached; keep it on your left and continue in a south-easterly direction, through newly planted trees and across a forest road, until you reach a gate in a wall, which you are reminded to shut after passing through. Go straight up the hill to meet the path along the top. If you are interested in ancient earthworks you might like to come back some hundreds of yards in order to explore the area of the hill fort and tumuli. But having explored, rested and admired the extensive views, the general direction is south. Keep to the path near the top fence round the wide sweep of the bay. The woods below are South Woods and beyond them, Southwood Hall and Southwood Farm. After nearly a mile of walking along the hill top, approaching the far headland, the path bifurcates. If you keep to the top one you would be following the line of the return journey of Walk No. 9, for views of Gormire, and it is well worth going on for a high level view of this lovely lake and Roulston Scar beyond, at a notice board denoting the Nature Reserve of the Yorkshire Naturalists Trust.

Since reaching the top at the Hill Fort, the route has been on the Cleveland Way and the White Rose Walk and it goes on at this level as far as Roulston Scar which is the headland in front, beyond Sutton Bank. But now we must retrace our steps to a point about 200 yards short of a post and wire fence. Then turn sharply downhill along an intrenchment which goes between rocks and a faint track leads down to the woods below. In the corner of the enclosing wall to the right and front there is a short fence and a gap which pass through on to a clearer trail through willow herb and young deciduous trees into the wood proper; then through bracken on the left hand side of the ditch, which is the ancient bridleway of Thirlby Bank. The clear track crosses, follows and recrosses the ditch until it reaches the Nature Reserve path near the bottom where a wooden sign says "Sloping path" with an arrow to the left but turn right here.

Coming out of the woods the path goes by trim lawns to a neat cottage. Turn right in front of it and go through a gate leading to a green lane northwards. From now on the hills will be on the right. In July the hedges here are covered with honeysuckle and at the corner of the next cross tracks there is a very fine lime tree, the scent from which almost surpasses that of the honeysuckle. Continue north towards Southwood Hall for 200 yards, where turn left at a grove of beech trees on a farm track, passing first through a wooden gate into a field and then an iron gate, leaving a small plantation on your right. Through the gate and continue forward along the visible line of a grubbed-out hedge to a barbed wire fence, at which turn right and follow the fence as far as a gate through the hedge ahead, into the next field and go through the middle on an old green track to the farm at Tang Hall.

Turn right and go over a cattle grid on to a country road, tarmacadamed to take each pair of motor car wheels towards a house that can be seen at the head of a little valley. When another cattle grid is reached there is a notice marked "Private Road". This means it is barred to cars but not to foot travellers because is is a right of way, so go on for a little over a hundred yards until the road curves round towards the farm. Leave it and go off to the left on a good farm track which leads to a depression between two wooded hills, which will have been noticed ahead for some little time. The cart track turns left to the south side of the western wood; leave it and go forward on a less pronounced cart track towards a gate at the other end of the field in the middle of the small valley. There used to be a right of way through this gate but the farmer had the route altered, and agreed upon, in order to keep a bull in the field. So bear off to the left hand corner where the new path goes just into the wood and skirts the field as far as a solid, two-gated bridge over a stream (Lunshaw Beck).

Over the bridge and into a field; ahead can be seen a small isolated farm building. Still on the right of way, go past it and through the gateway beyond on to a farm track, with the hedge on your right. Go through another gateway and another field; the hedge is now on your left, follow it to the gate which leads out of the field into the lane first taken out of Boltby, and so back to the village and the car.

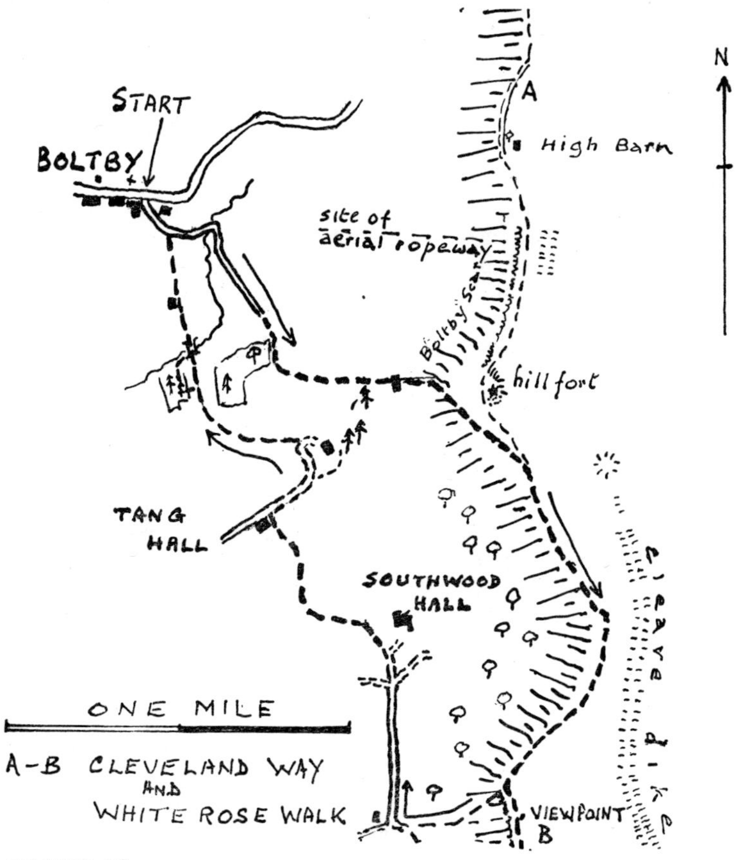

WALK 10

Walk 11 Boltby, Cowesby, Steeple Cross and Reservoir-12 miles (19 km)

ON this occasion there is a combination of the beauties of the valleys beneath the western escarpment, well-kept parkland in a peaceful situation, some bracken slopes and heather moors, and a return through the forest and by the side of the reservoir which from some aspects can be quite beautiful.

Some of the roads used today are on Forestry Commission land and are not legal rights of way: the Forestry Commission, however, welcomes walkers on their roads provided they are careful not to start fires or leave litter. Smokers please take especial care.

Although Boltby is the chosen start point, a start could equally well be made from Kirby Knowle, Cowesby or Kepwick. The routes out of Kirby Knowle and Cowesby are described below. If to cut into the route from Kepwick, take the bridle track through the field just east of the obelisk, starting at the second gate towards the village from the monument. Cross the field towards the top left hand corner where there are two gates. Take the upper, smaller one and go straight ahead until you reach the bridleway signpost. Go uphill from there.

From Boltby, by the millstone sign on the left hand side going in from the direction of Thirsk, there is a green track which follow into the field from which Ravensthorpe Manor can be seen, pass through two iron gates in fairly quick succession and in front of some farm buildings. The track leads you between the Manor and the stables, after which turn to the left behind the house on a track among rhododendrons and pass above the garden from which there are good views of Boltby, Roulston Scar and Hood Hill. Now taking a north-westerly direction the track leads below the hill where the spot height 907 is marked on the map. Thirsk and the Vale of Mowbray come into sight and on one notable occasion when the snow was on the tops of the Pennines, showing them up to the best advantage, one could observe well to the south the power stations of the West Riding, as well as York Minster, much nearer.

Keep to the bridle track below the edge of the moor which goes through the trees into a delightful valley, on the opposite side being the shapely knoll of Primrose Hill, and on to Kirby Knowle. The path comes out into the village nearly opposite the end of the road to Cowesby, which take. Although it is a motor road it is a quiet one, passing through a valley cut by meltwater from the receding glacier at the end of the last ice age. The land between trees on the left, above New Building, has been much used for camping by Scouts for many decades.

Nearing Cowesby, observe on the right the Hall and park beautifully enfolded in a bay below the moors. When in the village turn right on the bridle road to Helmsley, duly signposted, and soon you have the option of taking the sunken road to the left or bearing right into the woods above the Hall and taking the next track to the left signposted to Helmsley, which slopes upwards to a gate above the woods. If the sunken road towards Kepwick is taken (good for primrose and violets in season) go through the white gate at the end and on to the moor, keeping straight on as far as the bridle track signpost, where after observing the obelisk on Howe Hill at Kepwick, turn uphill on the zig-zag track and at the top (this is Pen Hill) cross the field to a white gate at the far corner of the wood; go through it on to a sheltered path between wall and wood. There is an equally good track on the other side of the wall for better views. At the end of the wood side path go through a gate on to the moor. This is the gate the short cut reaches.

Immediately ahead on the skyline there is a tumulus and a wall beneath it with a track immediately to the right of the wall; beyond and to the left is the forest and this is what we are making for. It is reached by keeping to the outside of Cowesby Hall wood until you reach a wooden gate in another wall in front of you. Go through it and keep between two walls on a track nearer to the left hand side one. The going is now straightforward until you cross a track just before reaching the forest. Bear left on it and go into the forest where the track will lead you quickly into an area recently cleared and which therefore gives impressive views to the south and protection by trees if the wind is in the north—a good place for lunch. The slightly rising track to the drove road makes a fine walk along the terrace so long as the area remains cleared. At Steeple Cross the old bridle road to Helmsley goes straight over the drove road but, from the crossing, it is no longer marked on the one-inch map. Antiquaries will want to visit the ancient Long Barrow, much older than the plentiful round barrows on the moors, and they will find it by crossing the moor towards the trig point at 1,234 feet.

The return is through Forestry Commission land. Turn back a few yards and take the first ride on the left which descends only slightly. Take the hairpin turn on the first road on the right downhill and cross the next road going straight on downhill on a dirt track. Turn left at the bottom and continue downhill, with the infant stream on your right, as far as the next road junction where you turn to the right, crossing to the right of the stream which is still only a trickle. Then take the next turn left and continue straight on where you pass another road on your right. Here start looking for the reservoir below, which you will soon see through the trees but you will only get a good view of it if you go beyond the dam and walk back to it. The road now naturally leads back to Boltby. It is possible to take paths across fields near Lunshaw House but at this stage of the day it is pleasant to step out on a straightforward track.

All the villages seen today have great beauty in their natural settings and all are typical of the district.

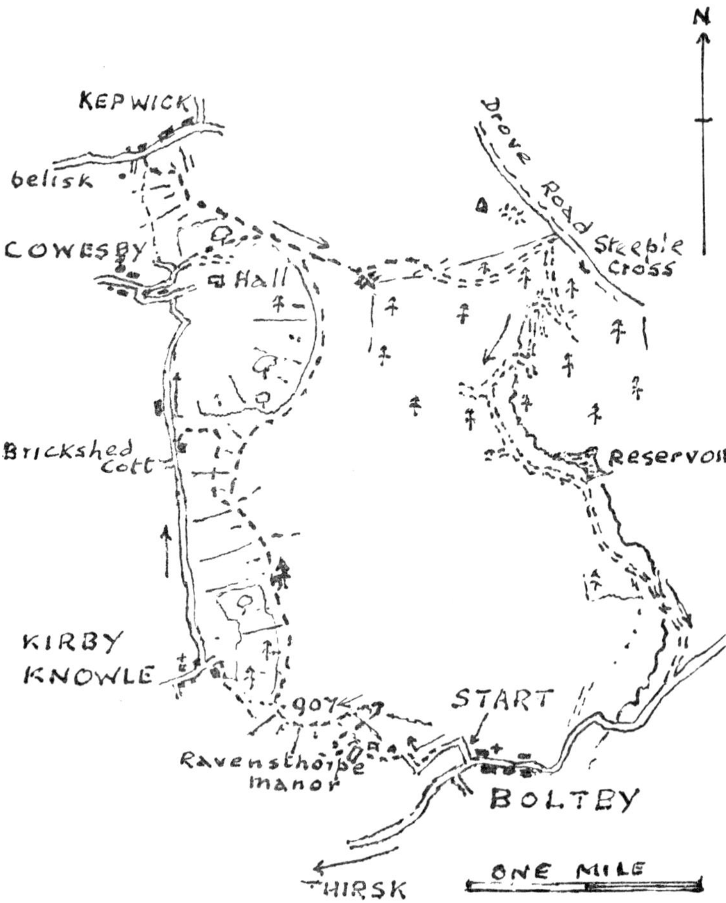

WALK 11

Walk 12 The Drove Road over Black Hambleton -7½ miles (12 km)

THE history of the old drovers' roads, used extensively to take cattle from Scotland to the south in the seventeenth and eighteenth centuries, makes an interesting study. One of the most romantic existed long before the Romans came; the drovers passing through Yarm on the way to Malton and York made full use of the high level route which entered the Clevelands at Scarth Nick, passed over the top (or nearly the top) of Black Hambleton and on to the region above Sutton Bank and beyond.

From the point of view of the walker, undoubtedly the best part of the road goes over Black Hambleton and round the top edge of the bay overlooking the Siltons and Kepwick. Long distance walkers approach today's section of the road either from the north or the south but a good circular route can begin at Kepwick. The start point is a sharp bend in the road, half a mile to the north of the village. Approaching it by car one can see above the start point an attractive knoll, Nab Plantation, the centre point of the re-entrant, green and outstanding in its setting below the russets of the slopes of the escarpment which embraces Black Hambleton.

Park the car near the gate with a sign of a horse on it and marked Nab House. Go on the farm road towards Nab Plantation. (The lower wood is French Hill Wood). Keep on the track to the farm where the right of way is on the right of the buildings and goes through the centre of the field beyond, leading to the left hand side of a stone wall and down to a bridge over a stream. Cross it and go uphill to a gate, beyond which is an old but well constructed kiln. Keep to the track, leaving the kiln on your left, until it reaches a stone wall. A small brick pump house is on the other side but do not cross to it, keep the wall on your right as you climb up Kepwick Moor. The Drove Road is reached at the top where their is a gate across it, at the site of an old inn, now in ruins, still shown on some maps as Lime Kiln House.

Turn left on the wide green expanse between walls and enjoy walking on the springy turf, with heather moor on your right and beautiful views on your left of the Vale of Mowbray and the distant Pennines, if the weather be clear, and locally Kepwick and the Siltons. The outlier near Over Silton is Carlow Hill.

At Whitestones—White Gill Head—take the left hand turn, still on the Drove Road, a clear track through the heather with a wall on your left. Be careful not to miss this turn, but if you do, you will find yourself on a track going over open moorland—so look out for the wall. The view to the north opens out as the road reaches the top of the hill. Immediately below is Osmotherley Moor; further on is the dip of Scarth Nick, and the bumps of the Lyke Wake Walk are to the right front.

The road now descends steeply off Black Hambleton and comes near to the conifers which will have been seen on the left for some little time. Before coming to the end of the trees look for the gate on the left and go over the stile by the side of it, going through the woods on a good forest ride. Keep to the main track, which is metalled, which soon goes down through trees by the side of Red Way Gill where the view opens out. After a mile of this forest road a gate is reached and you pass on to a long lane that has no turning until it descends steeply on to the Over Silton to Kepwick road, narrow and not much traffic on it. Nevertheless the safest way is to walk on the right and there is nearly a mile to the car.

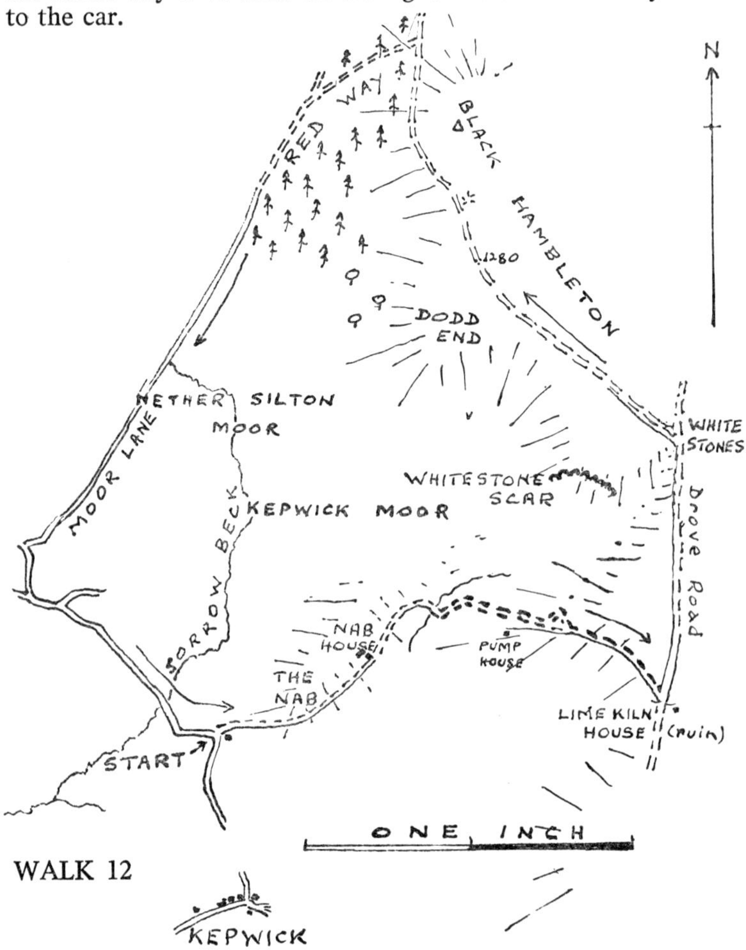

WALK 12

Walk 13 Osmotherly, Thimbleby Moor, Over Silton and Forest Road-9 miles (14·5 km)

THIS is a walk of great variety, incorporating parts of the Cleveland Way, a visit to the Hanging Stone above the village of Thimbleby, passing through the beautifully situated village of Over Silton, some lovely views of the bay in the hills and Kepwick Moor, a walk along part of the Drove Road below Black Hambleton and finally returning through the pleasant little valley of Oak Dale.

Osmotherley is a favourite holiday centre, well known as being near the start of the Lyke Wake Walk. The Cleveland Way passes through it and it is proposed today to leave the village on this track. Very close to the War Memorial in the centre of the village there is a ginnel* between two houses. Go through it, jinking slightly to the right, cross the back lane to a stile on which there is a moors path sign, and this takes you into a very narrow lane between a wall and a holly hedge. Go straight across the field beyond, to the gate opposite, beside which is a stone V stile, then bear slightly left on the track keeping 20 or 30 yards away from the hedge on the left. This takes you to the top of a wood and a well marked path leading down to the beck and over a good footbridge. Take the clear path opposite keeping to the side of the hedge. Go over a stile, cut across the field towards a gateway above the house, but go through a V stile in an electric fence and take the cart road between electric fences as far as the enclosed lane. Turn right and continue until you reach the motor road where you turn to the left, walk on it for less than 50 yards, then pass through a gateway on the right where there is an Acorn and a Moors Path sign. The track goes alongside the hedge to a gate, across a field to another gate on which is marked Oak Dale, and through the trees down to the level of the lake. Cross a bridge over an arm of the reservoir. The Cleveland Way goes straight on but leave it here by turning to the right just beyond a sign saying trespassers will be prosecuted. There is a right of way but do not leave the track which takes you along the top end of the reservoir, past a hut to a concrete bridge leading over the stream.

Take the track in front of you, after crossing, leading away from the beck and slope up the hill half right towards a small eight sided reservoir and a stone hut. Continue uphill in the same direction through bracken and sparse trees until you reach the corner of a mature wood, Big Wood. At the top, a slight track can

**A North-country word for a passage-way.*

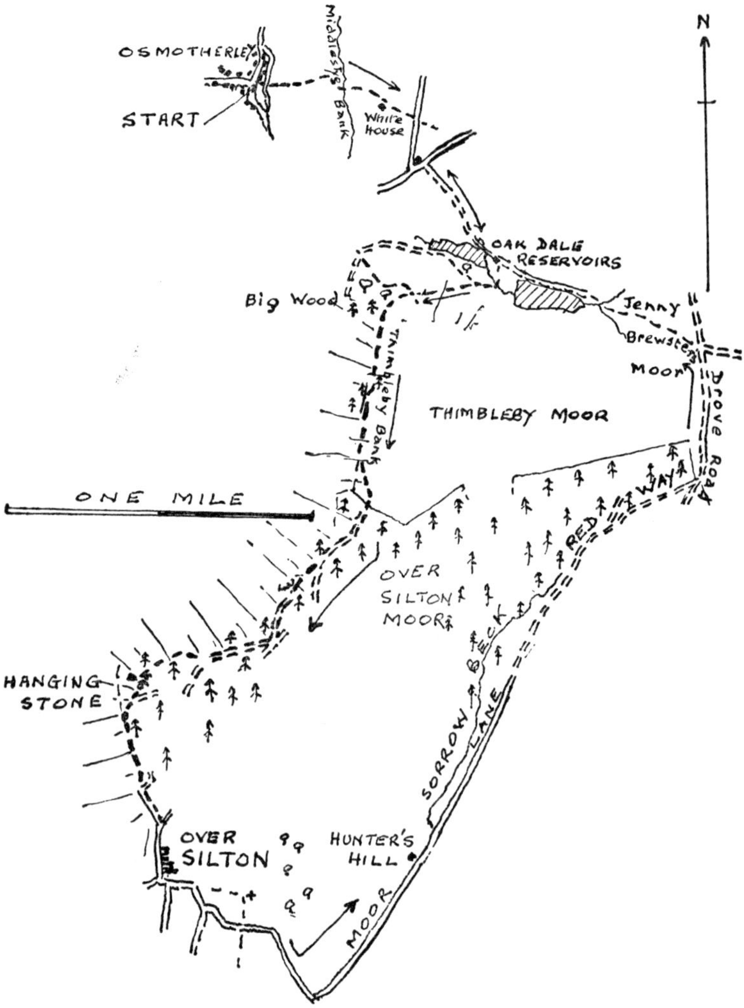

OSMOTHERLEY
START
Middlesty Bank
White House
N
OAK DALE RESERVOIRS
Big Wood
Jenny
Brewster
Moor
Thimbleby Bank
THIMBLEBY MOOR
Drove Road
ONE MILE
RED WAY
OVER SILTON MOOR
HANGING STONE
SORROW BECK
LANE
OVER SILTON
HUNTER'S HILL
MOOR

WALK 13

be seen coming up from inside the wood. Keep to the edge of the wood going far enough to the west to be able to get good views of the Vale of Mowbray and the Pennines in suitable weather, then turn south and find the track which keeps 50 yards or so below the edge of the moor and leads through a wall surrounding some fir trees and passes near the top of another clump of conifers. Keep to the edge of the moor on a track passing through bracken but before reaching the forest fence half a mile ahead start to climb slightly upwards to find a broad wooden stile over the fence and continue south on a grass covered ride through the trees. As the trees on the right thin out the ride continues along the edge of rocky cliffs — evidence of the sort of country in which to expect the Hanging Stone—but keep on the ride for several hundred yards until you reach another outcrop of rock and conifers again on the right of the ride. Here there is a narrow track on the right going over the top of the rocks; take it and continue on it to the right of the plantation until it leads naturally into another ride between trees, still keeping more or less to the same contour. Quite soon the track begins to rise slightly until it reaches a cross track and another ride which forms an arrow head with the one just traversed. Take this track to the right; after about half a mile the trees on the right thin out and after joining more trees on the right there is a narrow track leading to the right, which take; it passes over another rock outcrop. Turn left, continue in a general southerly direction on a narrow path through the trees, and keeping to the top edge of the cliff the Hanging Stone is reached. This is a high rock cleft from the main mass; the best views of it are from the village of Thimbleby and the track between; but that is for another day.

Take the track leading downhill just beyond the Stone to the ride below; turn left and keeping to the path just within the forest boundary—a 3 ft. stone pillar marks the path—come to the northern end of the village of Over Silton. You soon reach the southern end of it and at the road junction turn left towards Kepwick; keep on this narrow motor road for two-thirds of a mile and turn left up a steep bank in Moor Lane, a metalled straight road which after a mile reaches a gate into an extensive forest area.

The road within the forest is also metalled and this road has good wide verges to walk upon. It passes into a narrow valley and reaches the Old Drove Road coming down from Black Hambleton. Turn left on the Drove Road and as soon as it arrives at the motor road turn off to the left on the track leading down to the two reservoirs in Oak Dale which can be seen below. Beneath the bracken there is bog but this can be avoided by keeping on the high ground to the right for a little while. The path leads to the right of the top reservoir and soon joins the outward route, which follow back to Osmotherley.

Walk 14 Lady Chapel, Scarth Wood Moor and Scarth Nick-5 miles (8 km)

ON the road northwards out of Osmotherley towards Swainby nearly two miles out of the village and just beyond the reservoir, there is a favourite picnic spot known for miles around as Sheepwash, marked "Old Quarries" on the one-inch Ordnance Survey map. Hereabouts there is plenty of room to park the car and explore the local moors and stream. Those who want to go a little further may care to do a stretch of the Cleveland Way and see the start point of the famous Lyke Wake Walk on Scarth Wood Moor.

To reach the Cleveland Way route it is necessary to walk towards Osmotherley on the road by the side of the reservoir, by no means an unpleasant walk provided there are not too many cars about. At the top of the hill on the outskirts of the village there is a path to the right at the entrance to which are three signs: "Rueberry Lane", "To the Lady Chapel" and a "Moors Path" sign, indicating that this is where the Cleveland Way leaves the village. It is a good cart road leaving no doubt as to the way to go until a few hundred yards ahead there is a junction with a long-distance Acorn sign exactly midway between the two tracks. If you want to visit the Lady Chapel the right-hand, upper track is the one to take, leading to a hill which looks man-made, covered on its slopes with trees. The chapel is just over the hill and is worth a visit. It was erected by the Carthusian monks who lived in Mount Grace Priory situated lower down the hillside, but out of sight. The date is early sixteenth century but it has been extensively restored. (Some maps show "Lady's Chapel".)

Continuing northwards the track drops a little to meet a cross track. Go over a stile and turn right and you will soon pass through a new forest area above the line of the old trees on Swine Stye Hill. Keeping to the edge of the trees on the track you pass a television booster station near the site of an ancient signal station and this is Beacon Hill on Scarth Wood Moor. A white triangulation pillar, height 982 feet above sea level, denotes the start of the Lyke Wake Walk, a forty mile journey along the tops of the moors to Ravenscar on the coast. The journey we have taken from Osmotherley to this point is a little extra for good measure. To qualify as a dirger, a member of the Lyke Wake Club, one must do the walk in 24 hours. Let us now do the first mile of it!

The Cleveland Way joins the Lyke Wake Walk here and keeps

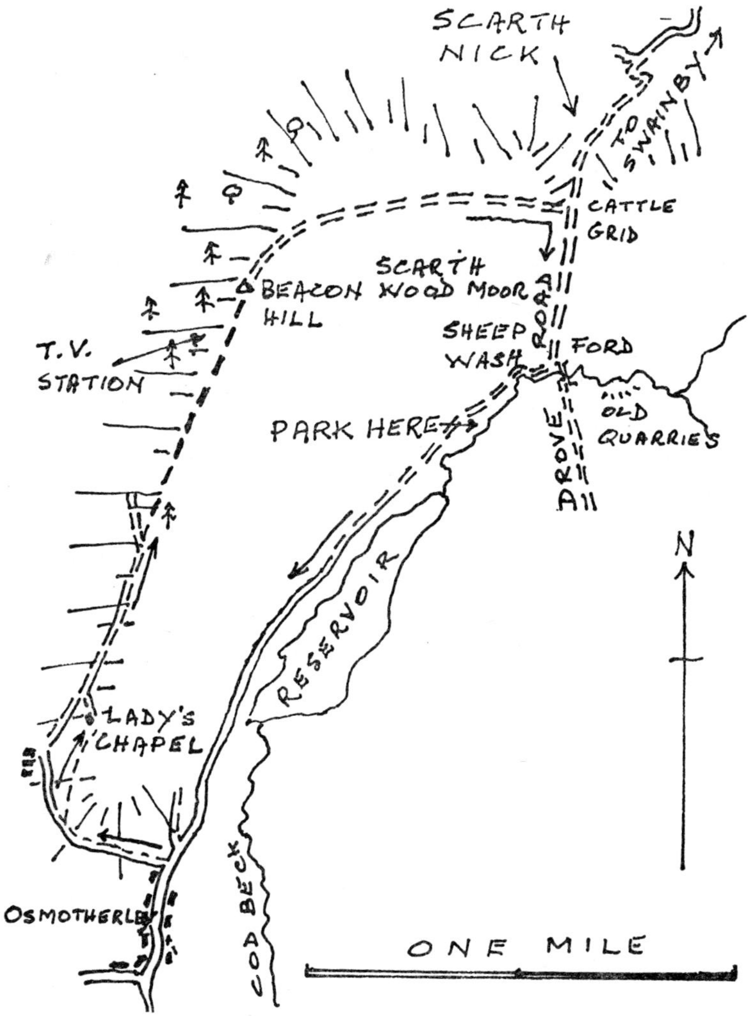
SCARTH NICK
TO SWAINBY
CATTLE GRID
SCARTH WOOD MOOR
BEACON HILL
T.V. STATION
SHEEP WASH
FORD
A19 ROAD
OLD QUARRIES
PARK HERE
ROVE A19
RESERVOIR
N
LADY'S CHAPEL
OSMOTHERLEY
COD BECK
ONE MILE

WALK 14

with it for 11 miles or so. From the trig point the wide track, now walked by about 6,000 people a year, leads away from the wood but continues generally in a northern direction across the moor. Go through a gate and downhill to Scarth Nick, a narrow cut in the hills gouged out by glacial meltwaters. Lyke Wake walkers cross the road at a cattle grid and continue to the Cleveland Hills on a path marked with a sign "Ravenscar 39 miles"! Instead of doing this, turn right up the road, which is the Drove Road, and this is the direction taken by those White Rose walkers who choose the long route. Half a mile further on they leave the road and cross the stream by the footbridge to continue on the Drove Road for many miles. Today's walkers will not do this but will rejoin their cars which should now be in sight.

It may just be that, having tasted the delights of an area which has attracted so many long distance walkers, the reader may be tempted sometime to follow in their footsteps.

Walk 15 Live Moor, Holey Moor, Carlton Moor and Scugdale-7miles (11km)

I REALLY believe that the best walking country in the National Park is over the "bumps" of the Lyke Wake Walk. These are the north-facing hills of the Clevelands which look so impressive when viewed from the road between Great Ayton and Stokesley. Conditions on the well-worn tracks among the heather are ideal for those who like to stride or stroll along the tops. The views of the Cleveland Plain below, with its patchwork of fields of all colours (especially at harvest time), the conical shape of Roseberry Topping in the middle distance, and Teesside beyond, all add to the joy of the local scene and the breadth of moorland air so easily accessible to so many.

The central feature of these hills is Cringle Moor and today's journey is intended to take in the three moors leading up to a good view of it and return via Scugdale, now a quiet pastoral valley but once a busy jet mining area. The signs of the mining activities are now very much subdued but it is interesting to observe the lines of the rock strata by the position of the old spoil heaps.

To reach the start point take the turning into Swainby off the main Stokesley-Thirsk road and go on either side of Scugdale Beck which flows through the village, pass to the right of the church and with the stream on your left; soon after leaving the village take the first left turn, sign-posted "Heathwaite Green" (Huthwaite Green on the Ordnance Survey maps); go along this by-road for just over a mile and look out for a telephone box on the left, opposite a road junction. Leave the car on the grass verge and go through the gateway where there should be an Acorn sign and a Moors Path sign denoting the Cleveland Way. There should also be a round black disc there but it had disappeared when I was last in Scugdale. These discs marked "L W W" appear frequently in this area and were put up on his land by Lord Ingleby, greatly helping dirgers and other walkers. The popularity of this part of the Lyke Wake Walk is shown by the organisers of both the Cleveland Way and the White Rose Walk (long route) choosing to go over the same ground.

Follow the well-used track past the old iron mine. Looking back and up the valley the jet mine spoil heaps can be seen from here. Go through a wicket gate and past lumps of old workings, now grass covered and sheep cropped. Skirt below the trees on your right and look out for a cut in the plantation and a black LWW disc. Take this steep route, where steps with wooden risers

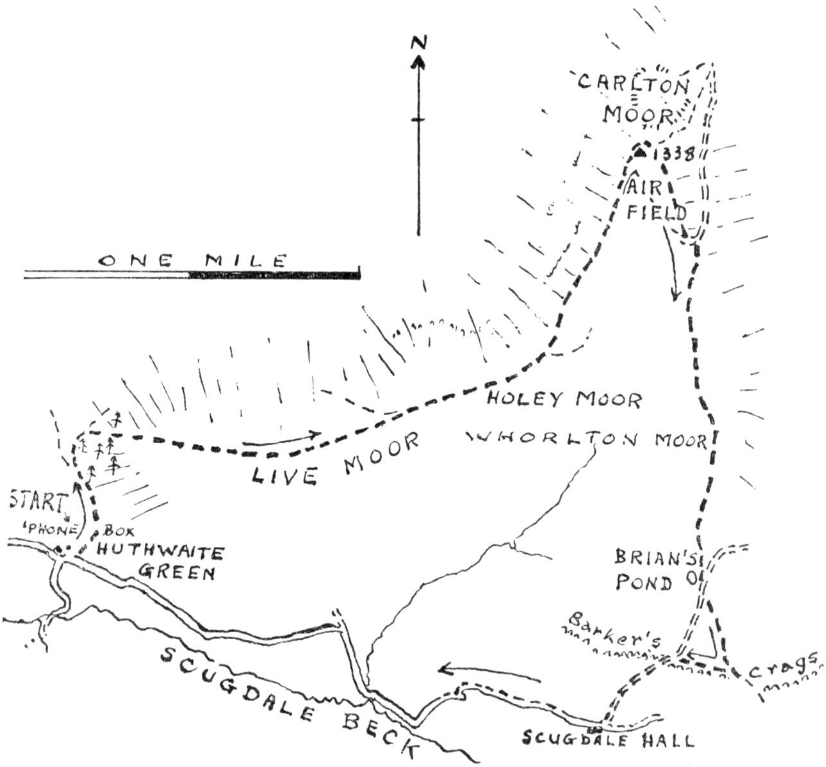
N
ONE MILE
CARLTON MOOR
1338
AIR FIELD
HOLEY MOOR
WHORLTON MOOR
LIVE MOOR
START
'PHONE BOX
HUTHWAITE GREEN
BRIAN'S POND
Barker's
Crags
SCUGDALE BECK
SCUGDALE HALL

WALK 15

and earth treads have been cut, leading to a good track on Live Moor, keeping to the moor top.

On the left can be seen the rounded outlier of Whorl Hill and to the right is Snotterdale, a branch of Scugdale. After passing a cairn on the top of Live Moor the ground dips a little and gently rises on to Holey Moor. There are paths to the left and then to the right but keep to the one near the steep edge and you will soon ascend to Carlton Moor which has been bulldozed for the use of the Newcastle Gliding Club. The track is on the edge of this bare surface and Carlton Bank is down below. Here shale from the old alum mines glows red, especially in the evening sun.

The culmination of the outward journey is at a triangulation pillar at 1,338 feet on the far left-hand corner of the airfield. From hereabouts there are the best of the views. Cringle Moor is across the steep dip ahead and between Carlton Moor and Cringle is the motor road up from Carlton and lots of space for car parking, which will be used for Walk No. 16.

Now there is to be a change of direction; still skirting the air-field turn due south. Soon the path joins a track for vehicles which bends and goes downhill but do not follow it down; at the hairpin bend go straight forward on the double green track in the heather. If not in mist the TV mast should be seen so keep in that general direction for the next two miles. There are some rocks ahead before leaving the vicinity of the gliding field; pass to the right of them and join a very clear track across the moor to Brian's Pond. The track is on the left of the pond and then bears to the right towards a rocky outcrop on the edge of Scugdale. For a fine general view of the district you could take the good alternative route ahead which also leads to the rocks, known as Barker's Crags. An upright boundary stone above the crags makes a good viewpoint. Scugdale is to the west, with Whorlton Moor both to the north and south of it. Straight ahead is Barker's Ridge leading to Green Howe; on the left is Raisdale, an arm of Bilsdale; and if you look back, away to the north-east between Cringle Moor and the next—which is Cold Moor—can be seen the Captain Cook's monument on Easby Moor.

Well-defined tracks along the top of the line of crags take one back to the path from Brian's Pond at a point where it takes a steep dip through the crags and then through bracken until it reaches the road at Scugdale Hall, now a tree nursery. The road is fit for motor traffic but as there is no exit at the head of the valley you should not be too much troubled with cars as you take the road down the two miles needed to reach Huthwaite Green.

Walk 16 Cringle Moor, Cold Moor, and Hasty Bank-7 miles (11 km)

THE walk now to be described would take a lot of beating anywhere in the country. It certainly is one of my favourites. Long-distance walkers may find themselves in this area too fatigued to take much notice of their surroundings; or they may be in the early stages of their journey and may even be walking in the dark. There are some arguments in favour of walking along these tops by the aid of a torch—the lights of Middlesbrough can be really impressive from here—but give me the daylight when one can put one's foot down firmly with little fear of a twisted ankle; give me the warmth of the sun, if not the midday, midsummer heat; and, most of all, give me the joy of looking about, observing the local scene and drinking in the distant views. So there is ample justification for spending a morning, an afternoon, an evening, or even the whole day, wandering about these lovely hills.

Three miles south-west of Stokesley, just off the main road, is the very fine village of Carlton-in-Cleveland. Motor up the village street and make for the hills. A mile out of the village there is a steep bank to climb on the road to Chop Gate; it is worth taking the car up for the views when you reach the top and there is plenty of good parking space, much used by supporters of long-distance walkers. These car driving supporters perform a very useful service to the walkers, carrying their food and spare clothing and providing an emergency party for any who fall by the wayside. Here, too, the motorist-walker may park his car. Up above is the airfield visited on Walk No. 15 and in the opposite direction, east, is Cringle Moor, the first objective.

Walk towards it on a well-trodden, well-cropped, green track past a small plantation and a plaque in memory of Alec and Annie Falconer "who loved these hills". An interesting diversion before making for the wallside and the ascent of Cringle would be to go towards the edge of the moor to the north to have a look at the big square rock known as the Three Lords Stone, the meeting point of three old estates.

Resuming the walk towards Cringle the path goes straight up on the right-hand side of a wall and on the top skirts round the northern edge, where a substantial wind shelter has been built (for about three people) in front of which there is a direction finder dedicated to Alec Falconer. The views are similar to those described in the previous walk but Roseberry Topping is nearer. The start point for the White Rose Walk is just below it and the whole of the wide sweep of the northern part of the walk can be seen from here, all along the tops of the moors. Looking north, the highest point of Cringle Moor (1,427 feet and the highest of the group) is about a quarter of a mile behind but it is not much higher than the present position and there is little to be gained by going inland. Instead, the track keeps to the moor edge above some crags and soon begins to descend steeply towards Cold Moor, the next top to attack. Drop down to the dip below, past some slag heaps on the left and on reaching two upright stones, previously used as gateposts, bear to the right through a gateway and round the end of a wall where there is an Acorn sign of the Cleveland Way and climb steeply to the top of Cold Moor to its highest point on the northern edge, 1,317 feet.

As on Cringle, the path on Cold Moor keeps nearly to the left-hand edge and ahead will soon be seen the Wainstones on Hasty Bank; the steep path will take you down and up to them where you may be able to see rock climbers practising their strenuous activities. The climbs include clefts, faces and even a needle.

The tendency so far will have been for the eye to wander to the left over the Cleveland Plain but at the Wainstones the view is to the right. Bilsdale is to the south, and to the south-east is Urra Moor where there is the highest point on the North York Moors, marked by a triangulation pillar at 1,489 feet.

To complete the outward journey go over the top of Hasty Bank and steeply down towards the Bilsdale road, the main road from Stokesley to Helmsley. Go over a stile into forestry land but there is no need to go on to the road unless you want to do so. One good reason for going on the road would be to obtain refreshment at a tea booth, a few hundred yards to the north, on a car park at the top of Clay Bank. Incidentally, this good car park would make an alternative start point for the walk. Curl round the end of Hasty Bank on a Forestry track and you will soon find yourself facing the way you have come but now you will see the cliffs of Raven's Scar in front and above. Keep on the track above the trees of Broughton Plantation—the village down below to the right is Broughton. The path is an old jet miners' track which keeps pretty level round Hasty Bank until you can see the Wainstones on your left. Go through a gate on which there is a notice asking you to keep it shut and reads "Keap sheap owt".

The track continues to the side of Cold Moor on more or less the same level, still above the trees, and emerges at the gap between Cold and Cringle Moors where there is a stile. Pass the upright stones which were passed on the outward journey and go over to the shale heaps below Cringle Moor, once again bearing to the right of the moor, this time on a narrower path but still maintaining the same level. The path bends round a projection of Cringle Moor and as you round the bend you will see Carlton Bank ahead. Continue on the path round to the left and join the outward track not far away from where you left the car.

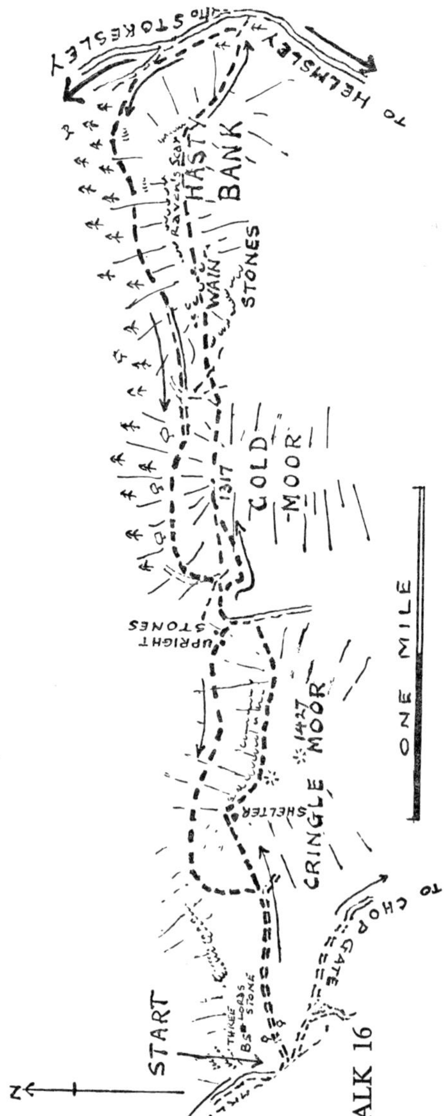

Byland Abbey.

Walk 7

White Rose Walkers near Sutton Bank, Gormire.

Walk 9

Whitestone Cliff.

Walk 9

Primrose Hill, Kirby Knowle.

Walk 11

Nab Plantation and Black Hambleton from Kepwick.

Walk 12

View from Scarth Nick.

Walk 14

In Bilsdale.

Walk 17

Bloworth Crossing.

Walk 22

Walk 17 Seave Green, Urra Moor, Ancient Stones and Earthworks-8¾ miles (14 km)

HERE is an opportunity to take in many places of interest—the prehistoric earthworks which Bill Cowley tells us in his book "Lyke Wake Walk" are known locally as Cromwell's Trenches; the highest point on the North York Moors on Round Hill at Bottom Head, 1,489 feet; some old boundary stones; and a short stretch where meet the Cleveland Way and all the alternative routes of the Lyke Wake and White Rose Walks.

The chosen start point is the village of Seave Green but the car park south of Chop Gate may be preferred, in which case the route to the top via William Beck Farm is recommended, with a return from Seave Green by main road or footpath making the total mileage a nice round ten.

From the main road at Seave Green go over the bridge and turn right immediately, ford the stream and turn left up the right hand side of it (the true left bank) on a stone trod which leads on to a cart road, which follow, cross another ford and keep on the cart road up the hill to a farm. The track passes between two lovely little valleys, the one on the left being the way to come back. Pass to the left of the farm buildings where the track keeps to the right of the fence in the field beyond and on either side of the wall in the further field. Ahead are some old workings and new afforestation enclosed by a wire fence over which is a stile. Go over it and keep just within the fence, still going straight uphill until reaching an old mine road now utilised by foresters. Turn right and go gently uphill for about 200 yards where the wide track continues forward but take the older track to the left, climbing more steeply to another wide track. Turn left and go gently upwards. In the middle distance there is some fine rock scenery. Take the right hand elbow for 50 yards when you come to the wall of the forest. Turn left up a grass track as far as a gate which pass through and scramble up the gully on your right to the moor top.

Immediately you are upon the earthworks, alongside which is a good track. Turn left on it and enjoy some straightforward walking and excellent views of Bilsdale, until you reach the other track coming up from Seave Green. Here leave the earthworks for the time being, turning right on to the wide bulldozed track leading over the moor. This is on the popular route of the White Rose Walk and an alternative Lyke Wake route but not now so much used by dirgers as it was in the early days of the Walk. One-and-

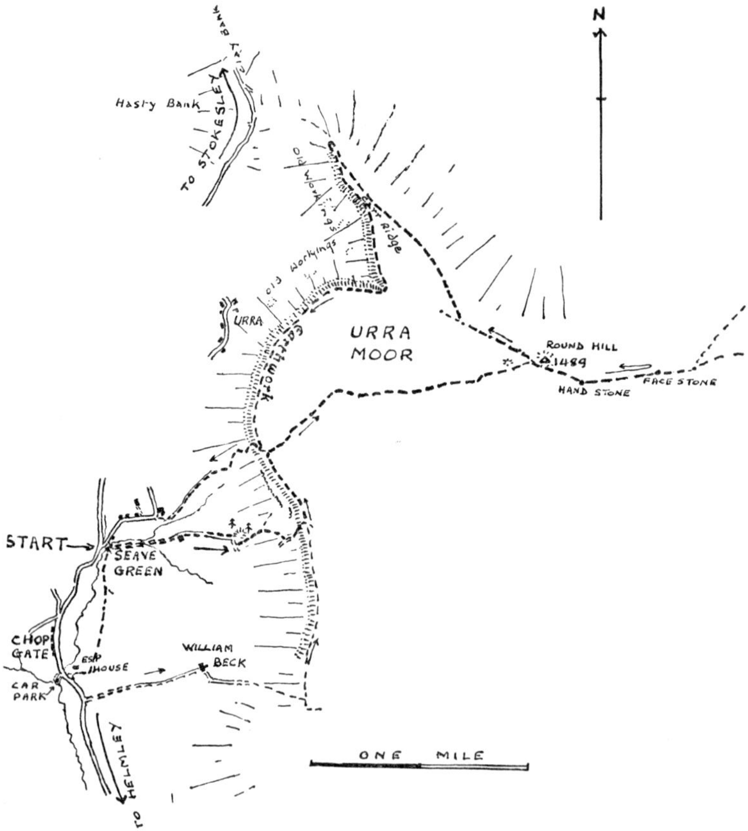
N
TO STOKESLEY
Hasty Bank
Clay Bank
Old Workings
Cock Ridge
Old Workings
URRA
Earthwork
URRA
MOOR
ROUND HILL
1489
HAND STONE
FACE STONE
START
SEAVE
GREEN
CHOP
GATE
ESP
HOUSE
WILLIAM
BECK
CAR
PARK
TO HELMSLEY
ONE MILE

WALK 17

a-half miles on this wide track brings you to a conical cairn on the left and, fifty yards further on, to the junction with a similar track coming in from the left. This is the point at which all the long-distance routes meet. It is often very misty here when the cairn between the routes cannot be seen but the identity of the junction can be confirmed by observing a short standing boundary stone on the north side of the ride. On it are carved the initials AM and traced on the west- and east-facing sides are white acorns denoting the Cleveland Way. Just to the east of the stone is a wooden post on which is marked LWW. If the weather is clear the white triangulation pillar shows on the tumulus of Round Hill; it is worth taking the narrow track to it in order to stand on the highest point in the National Park, then back to the main track where another boundary stone can be seen. This is the Hand Stone; a hand carved on the south face points to the east and says "This is the way to KIR" (Kirbymoorside) and on the other side the hand faces west with the words "This is the way to STO" (Stokesley). 300 yards further east is the Face Stone on which, facing east, is carved a face, and on the top KIR.

Now retrace your steps to the junction where all the long-distance walks meet and bear to the right, returning along the Lyke Wake classic route; along it are many boundary stones beside the bulldozed track for nearly a mile, then there is a turn to the right on to an older footpath where the footprints of walkers will be seen in the black peaty soil. There is a sign LWW at this junction. Continue on the Lyke Wake route along the nab until about half a mile from the main road where the land begins to fall away steeply, then look for the trench and mound of the earthworks. This nab is called Carr Ridge; turn sharply back left and take the good track along the earthwork keeping roughly to the same contour all along the moor edge and it therefore recedes into a ravine soon to be reached. Here rises the infant Bilsdale Beck. Where the path emerges from this little valley there is an outcrop of rocks. If you scramble to the top you will be rewarded by good views of the scene below; some signs of old workings all along at a lower level; the four farms of the village of Urra; a profile of the Wainstones at the far end of Hasty Bank on the opposite side of Bilsdale; and a comprehensive view of the top end of this lovely valley.

Soon after passing the village below, a wall cuts into the earthworks. Keep above it until you come to the road leading down to Seave Green. Turn down it, passing Bilsdale Hall and other typical houses built of the local sandstone, all having well-kept, colourful gardens. Soon you are back at the start point.

If you wish to return to the car park below Chop Gate by the field path, turn left just before the bridge leading to the main road, ford the stream and keep straight on for Esp House.

Walk 18 Tripsdale-5 miles (8 km)

PLENTY of time should be allowed to explore the little-known valley of Tripsdale which is crossed on the way to Bransdale (via Stump Cross) from Chop Gate or Seave Green in Bilsdale. The dale is craggy and uninhabited and in it there is a clear crystal beck which could allow a plunge if not a swim. The crags are sometimes used for climbing training.

Approaches from the lower end of the valley can be impeded by thick and high bracken so the best way to get there is from higher up Bilsdale even though a stiff ascent is involved.

Near the bridge to the south of Chop Gate is a sign-post reading "Footpath to Snilesworth" and another "Car Park and Toilets". Leave the car here and turn right on the main road; walk on it for 300 yards and turn left through a gateway on a farm road sign-posted "Footpath to Bransdale". Follow it, passing the front of William Beck Farm, into a wet lane leading upwards to a field and the open moor. Continue upwards in the same direction until you reach a tractor trail at the top on which turn right and quickly left to go over the top of the moor on a bulldozed track.

This is Nab End Moor and over to the right will be seen the stone cairn in the area of the Bridestones (not to be confused with the more famous and more dramatic Bridestones near Staindale). Ahead, on the moor beyond the valley, will be seen the old bridle track to Bransdale, not included in today's walk.

The bulldozed part of the track comes to an end at the edge of the moor where there is a pretty comprehensive view of Tripsdale; a clear track zig-zags down to the beck. At the turning on to the last "zag" above the trees and the beck, note the sloping track to the left which will be the route of the return journey. Go down to the ford and linger at leisure around this lovely green spot amid the trees and the surrounding bracken and heather moors.

On the return journey go straight ahead at the first corner through the heather on a track which is sometimes concealed but the direction is clear. At a cross track, which goes down to the right front into the head of Tripsdale but which is not yet a right of way, there is a notice board indicating "Bransdale Footpath" with an arrow pointing to the way we have come. Continue sloping up the hill in the same direction for 150 yards; turn up left to the top of the moor, passing shooting butts by the right-hand side of the track. Near the top, on the left, are the remains of an aircraft which, sadly, just failed to skim the highest part of the

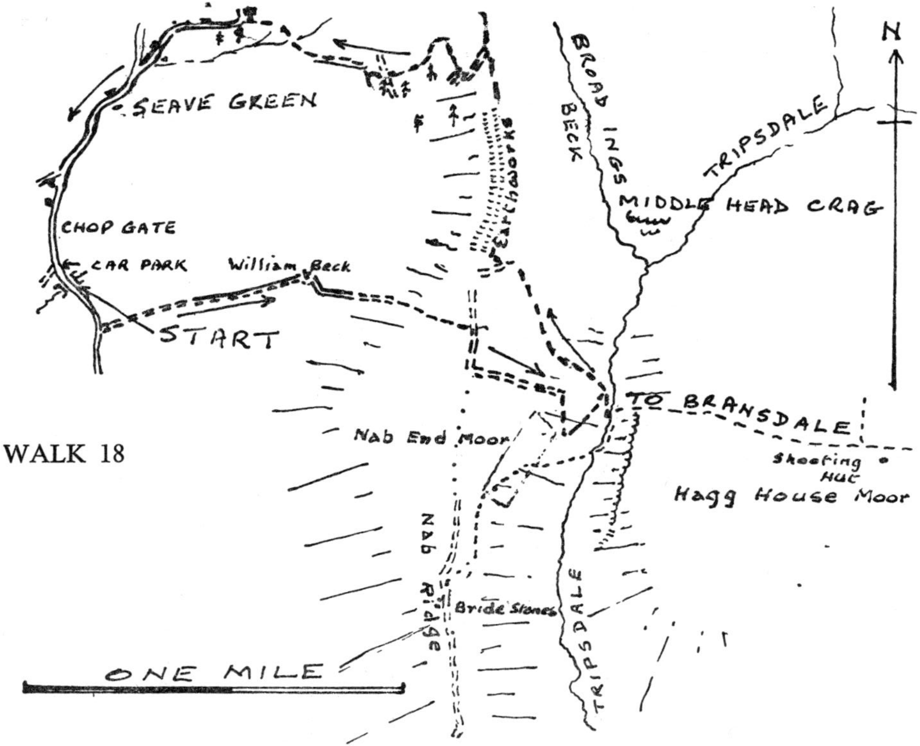
N
SEAVE GREEN
CHOP GATE
CAR PARK
William Beck
START
Earthworks
BROAD INGS
BECK
TRIPSDALE
MIDDLE HEAD CRAG
TO BRANSDALE
Shooting Hut
Hagg House Moor
Nab End Moor
Nab Ridge
Bride Stones
TRIPSDALE
ONE MILE

WALK 18

moor. The clear track passes more shooting butts and standing stones at intervals, all on the right, near the track. To the left front is the TV mast on the other side of Bilsdale. Reaching the edge of the moor, turn right on a good track which goes along the earthworks and gives one an opportunity to see the head of Bilsdale, chiefly Hasty Bank with the Wainstones jutting out on the left of the moor. Walk for half a mile on this excellent track. Down below are some crags; a forest plantation through which we shall soon pass; evidence of former mining; and lower down, Seave Green with a green wooden building at the top, which is the next objective.

Pass a track on the right where a notice reads "No Footpath"; 100 yards further on go down a gully on the left to a gate leading to the plantation. Go through it and keep on the main forest track taking the first hairpin bend, to the right, but leaving the main track at the second hairpin bend (which this time goes to the left) but our route is straight on, the way being a little narrower but still a good green track which winds steadily downhill through the trees until a straight shale path is joined. Jink a few yards to the left on this and then continue downhill on a faint track through the trees, keeping a wall on your left hand side. Go over a stile at the bottom of the wood, bear slightly right and go through a gate into a field, keeping a stone wall on your left. Through the gateway at the bottom of the field, immediately turn right through a small gate into a rough pasture where a faint track takes you above a spring, down a valley to a V stile in the wall near the bottom.

On the other side of the valley a clear, sloping path leads upwards to a gate into a lane near the green wooden building, above some old conifers. Turn left in it and soon pass through a gateway on to the small motor road by the side of Bilsdale Hall. Turn left and go downhill by the side of the houses and lovely gardens of Town Green to the main Bilsdale Road at Seave Green. Turn left and walk through Chop Gate, pass the shop and the pub, for return to the car park.

Walk 19 Roppa Plantation and Helmsley Moor -6 miles (9·5 km)

ONE of the joys of today's journey is its simplicity. From the start point above Helmsley Bank the whole of the walk can be surveyed showing a good mixture of forest and moorland. The going is good all the way and one should be able to return home with dry feet. The coach road and the Hanging Stone both provide interest for the antiquary and the casual visitor. If necessary, the distance may be reduced to four and a quarter miles by cutting out the moorland extension to the Hanging Stone.

To reach Helmsley Bank by car take the road in Helmsley between the church and the Feversham Arms; 200 yards ahead turn left at a sign indicating No Through Road (leaving the old graveyard on your right) and keep to the tarred road north for four miles. This involves passing two farms, three gates, only one of which may have to be opened and closed again, through a glade of old conifers to the open moor on the left front and a conifer plantation on the immediate right of the road. Pass through another gateway and on reaching the fifth gate, which is at the end of the plantation, park the car on the cropped grass among the heather. There is a grand view from here, Helmsley Bank, which is the start of the walk. This is the northern edge of the tabular hills so characteristic of the whole of the southern boundary of the National Park. The rock beneath our feet is coralline limestone whereas away to the north the rock is chiefly sandstone, a base on which the heather thrives. Looking north towards the television mast on Bilsdale West Moor, the purple heather on Helmsley Moor below us contrasts vividly with the greens of the forests and the browns of the bracken. Here, too, is to be seen a sculpture by Austin Wright, erected in 1977. It consists of two huge irregular metal Ds. Its purpose was said to be "to enhance the view" but it was the subject of controversy and press correspondence.

To the left, towards a triangulation pillar and to the right into more forests, there are good walks along the edge of the escarpment but our route today takes us straight on, sloping to the left down Helmsley Bank from which the whole of today's route may be seen: the track through the trees and moor to a ruin and the tumuli beyond; the two farms which will be skirted on the way to East Moor Wood; and the trail back through Roppa Plantation which is seen below and to the right.

At the bottom of the steep slope the tarred road ends at forest cross tracks and this is the point to which we shall return via the

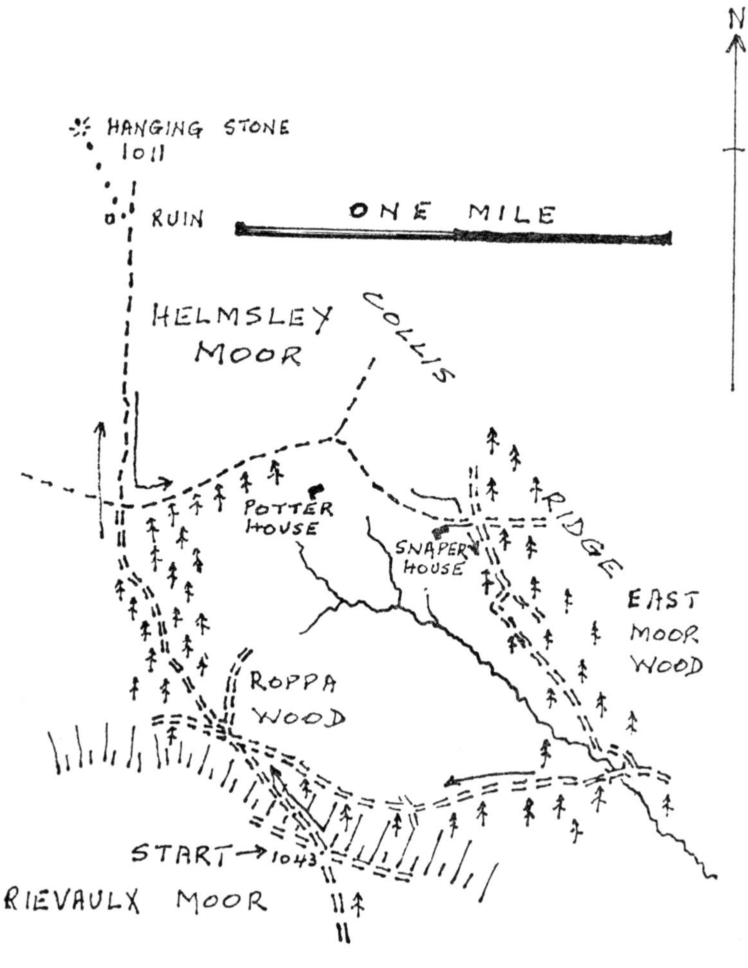
HANGING STONE
1011
RUIN
ONE MILE
N
HELMSLEY
MOOR
COLLIS
RIDGE
POTTER
HOUSE
SNAPER
HOUSE
EAST
MOOR
WOOD
ROPPA
WOOD
START
1043
RIEVAULX MOOR

WALK 19

trail on the right. It will be seen that there is car parking space here but to bring the car down here is not recommended because (*a*) due regard has been given for the car brakes and engine, (*b*) the views from Helmsley Bank can be much better appreciated walking than from a car and (*c*) there is a great sense of achievement (and relief) on reaching the car at the top of the hill at the end of the day.

Continue past the cross track for 20 paces and bear left on a forest track. Motoring from Helmsley and now on the forest track, the route has been on the old coach road to Stokesley which joins the Bilsdale road just short of Grange, and it is intended to continue on it on the moor ahead, although one may wonder how the coaches managed to keep upright in such bumpy country. When the forest track on this ancient route was being excavated a small horseshoe of the type used by the coach horses was found and is in the possession of the farmer at Potter House nearby, formerly a pottery. Walking through the trees, through forest rides to the right front can be seen on the moor the ruin which is on our line of march, and on emerging from the trees the view to the left opens out to reveal Easterside Hill and the moors beyond Bilsdale.

Leave the forest area through a gate and note a good cross track left and right to which we shall return, but now go straight on on an indistinct path which at first leads between two trenches. Believe it or not, one of these depressions is the old coach road. Follow its course and note the stone cairns on its side here and there. When the path turns leftish towards the ruin previously observed, it will be seen that the building was formerly a blast shelter, evidence of army activities during World War Two. The area has been pretty thoroughly cleared since those days but the reader is warned not to handle anything which might possibly be explosive.

To the north of the ruin will be seen a group of tumuli of the bronze age and in the centre of one of the cairns, 20 feet in diameter, rises the Hanging Stone. Eleven feet high, it leans towards the north-west and a stone cairn has been built on its tip. The height above sea level is 1,011 feet.

The stone is at the highest point near the junction of three parish boundaries. It is mentioned in books of reference but I have been unable to find out any history and can only conclude it is a gigantic boundary stone. Views from here are chiefly of ridge upon ridge of heather-clad high moors beyond Bransdale to the east and Bilsdale to the west.

Retracing one's steps to the forest gate, turn left on the clear track which never gets further than 200 yards from the plantation on the right and make towards the first farm, which is Potter House, but keep a field away from it and when the main track curves away to the left, leave it and keep to the side of the post and wire fence until you reach a gateway, which pass through. Take the faint path through the short grass and heather towards the next farm, Snaper House. Pass through the gate immediately above the farm, which is not occupied, and bear left, keeping a stone wall on your right. At the end of the wall turn right on to and open grassy tractor trail.

Here are very good views of the hills from which we started the walk. The trail leads through a gate into East Moor Wood on Collis Ridge; after about 400 yards of good going through a forest ride the road takes a big double bend, first right and then left downhill on an earth road through a wide ride. In the valley bottom there is a metalled (not tarred) road and a bridge over the stream with a Forestry Commission notice saying "Warning—Maximum Load 20 tons Gross." Turn right and go over the bridge (unless you have been putting on weight lately).

Continue uphill on this metalled road, ignoring side roads. The views open out first to the right and then to the left and soon ahead can be seen the line of the route back up Helmsley Bank, indicated by telegraph poles. Eventually the cross roads (or five road ends) will be reached and these should be recognised. Turn left up the hill, pausing from time to time, not only to regain breath but also to recapture the enjoyment of the day.

THE HANGING STONE, HELMSLEY MOOR

Walk 20 Riccal Dale-6½ miles (10·5 km)

RICCAL DALE is a lovely tree-clad valley, worth a visit at any time of the year but especially beautiful in autumn. After rain, the rights of way in the valley can be somewhat muddy but the alternative forest roads offer a route to keep the feet dry. These tracks are not all on rights of way but are available to walkers (but not motorists) by courtesy of the Forestry Commission.

The intention is to go up the valley at stream level on the true right bank (which is the left hand side going up), varied a little at the beginning by the crossing of the stream bed for a short distance, and returning on the other side, first at the top and later at stream level, finally there will be a mile of walking on the right bank again.

A feature of the rivers and streams coming down from the moors and cutting through the tabular hills is that in dry weather they sink below the stream bed and come up again at kelds a mile or more lower down. The River Riccal is no exception; it is quite probable a walker will find the river bed dry at the beginning and the end of the walk, in which case it is interesting to speculate on where the sound of rippling water will be heard, higher up the valley.

Take the Kirbymoorside road out of Helmsley and after a little more than a mile park the car on the grass verge just before the first bridge (Riccal Bridge). Go through the gateway on the left on a track leading through trees into a field. The next mile could be simplified by taking the forest track through the gate which will be seen ahead, but assuming the ground to be reasonably dry keep to the right of way through the field. It passes to the left of the trees ahead and goes towards the stream in the next field where the track passes over the river bed. If there is water in it, look for a fallen tree used as a bridge with another one for a balustrade. So, after a quarter of a mile from the start you have already crossed to the other side but only for a short time. Go through a gateway on a clear track through scrub, into the trees. Emerging from the trees the path goes through willow herb and the open view gives one an opportunity to admire the colours of the different kinds of trees all round. Now cross a good plank bridge and climb up to the forest track a few feet above. Those who have taken the easy way will have reached this point by keeping to the track along the valley bottom.

The going is good along the forest road for the next mile. On the left the trees are birch and oak and on the other side mixed conifers and, later, silver birches, which if seen against autumn colours look almost blue. As one approaches the level of the birches the sound of running water can be heard and, as road and stream come together, there is the water flowing freely. The road rises somewhat but is still within sight and sound of the water through the trees; the track levels out again and emerges from the trees with more views of the wider valley ahead. Soon on the right, down a side track, a shooting hut comes into sight; the side track leads to a low concrete bridge over the river—a good place for a picnic—but return to the trail over which you have been walking and continue up-valley but do not continue on the road, which goes up-hill; instead go forward on a good footpath through the woods, soon joining the river bank and very pleasant it is, too. But then there is some mud to negotiate, after which the path gets back to the road and the valley opens out again past a clearing on the left and a tree-clad nab can be seen ahead. Reaching the trees, the green track soon comes to the blunt end of a hairpin bend on a metalled forest road; take the turn down to the right and at the next junction take the right-hand alternative, over another solid-looking low concrete bridge; bear left and climb steadily up the forest road until Hasty Bank Farm can be seen through the trees below. Here will be seen on the right a clear footpath doubling back but continuing up-hill; but before taking this track it is worth going on for 80 yards for a good view across to the country visited in Walk No. 19. Return to the upward path through the trees and climb steadily until you reach a cart track above the tree line at the rim of the valley.

Turn right on the cart track, a good green road above the trees. Gorse is on the left and soon Oxclose Farm will be seen a field away. One or two tracks lead down through the trees but keep to the top for about a mile. The views hereabouts are somewhat restricted but the walk is pleasant enough and the scent of the trees adds to the pleasure. Eventually the view opens out and the wolds can be seen across the Vale of Pickering; but then the track begins to descend into the woods and joins another one coming in from the right. Bear left, and keep on the track at this level.

Immediately past a wooden pheasant rearing house there will be seen a path coming in from the left and two tracks ahead; take the left-hand path ahead, going down-hill, keeping to the main path (there are two side tracks on the left). Nearly at the valley bottom, turn left on a cross track and go through a gate, a clearing and another gate. Keep on a good green path through the bracken until you reach the level of some birch trees on the left and here look for a good metal footbridge over the river. The better path on the other side goes to the right for less than 100 yards where it joins the forest road on which the outward journey was taken. Turn left and continue down the valley on this track. Soon the main track turns upwards but keep to the valley floor for the last mile of this walk until you reach the gate at the end of the forest trail leading to the field entered at the beginning. Cross it to the last gate and the car.

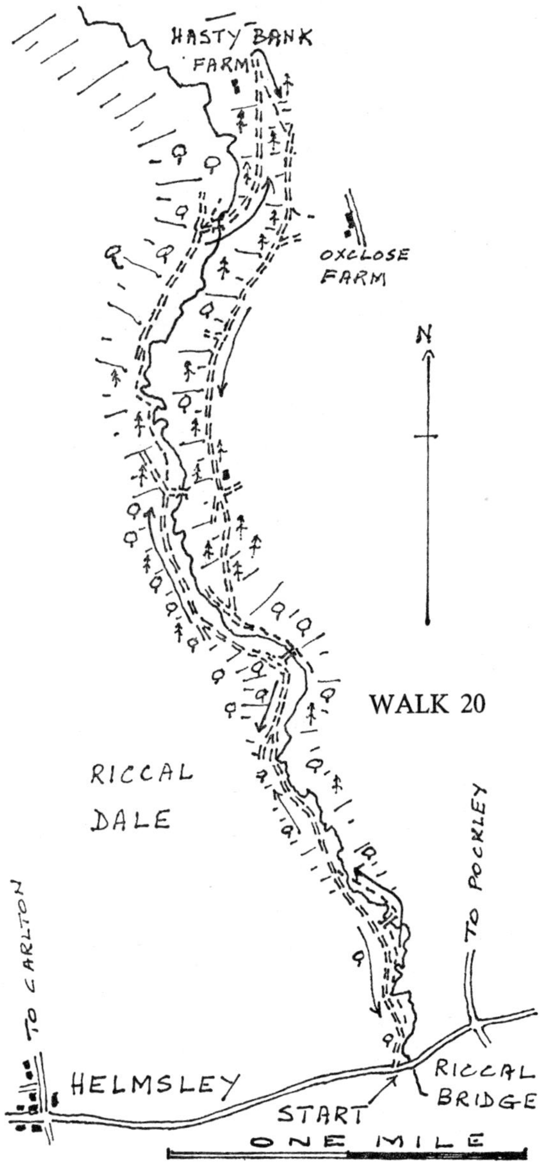

WALK 20

Walk 21 Stump Cross, Bransdale-3 miles (4·8 km)

With an optional extra at COWHOUSE BANK of any distance up to 8 miles (13 km.)

THE chief aim today is to take a moorland walk along good tracks to a position giving extensive views of the high moors and closer views of Bransdale.

Motoring out of Hemsley on the Scarborough (Kirbymoorside) road, turn left for the pretty village of Carlton before leaving the houses. A mile to the north of Carlton the road reaches a very fine viewpoint at Cowhouse Bank so before continuing towards Bransdale by car, turn in to the left where there is a signpost which reads "Footpath to Newgate Bank". There is plenty of room to park the car. This is another of those places on the edge of the tabular hills always worth pausing at for the almost unlimited views they give to the north. To the left front is Helmsley Moor with Roppa Plantation below it and East Moor Wood to the right of that. Above the trees straight ahead are the moors of Bransdale: East Moors, Pockley Moor, both of which we shall cross by car, and Bilsdale East Moor, on which we shall be walking later in the day. Over to the right is Birk Nab and the valley still further to the right is Riccal Dale.,

The walk of the day being only a short one, the reader may be tempted to investigate the footpath directed by the signpost, all of it being on good forest roads and tracks, giving many good views over to the right, going out, except where obliterated by trees. The rule is: keep to the path along the edge and do not go downhill. For the full distance pass Helmsley Bank (Walk No. 19); the triangulation pillar beyond (at 1,078 feet); to Newgate Bank (where a pause is recommended in Walk No. 3) four miles away, and return by the same route. The distance may therefore be shortened according to taste. Such simple directions hardly justify a separate chapter but if there is insufficient time to do the trip today it could be borne in mind for the future.

Resuming the car journey, go down Cowhouse Bank and enjoy five miles of moorland motoring until sighting the top end of Bransdale. Before the road turns downhill there is a signpost on the left saying "Footpath to Bilsdale". Leave the car here by the side of a good moor road liberally scattered with white stone for the first half mile (thereafter it is a sandy track). Pass a sign indicating no access for motor vehicles and then on the left at fairly

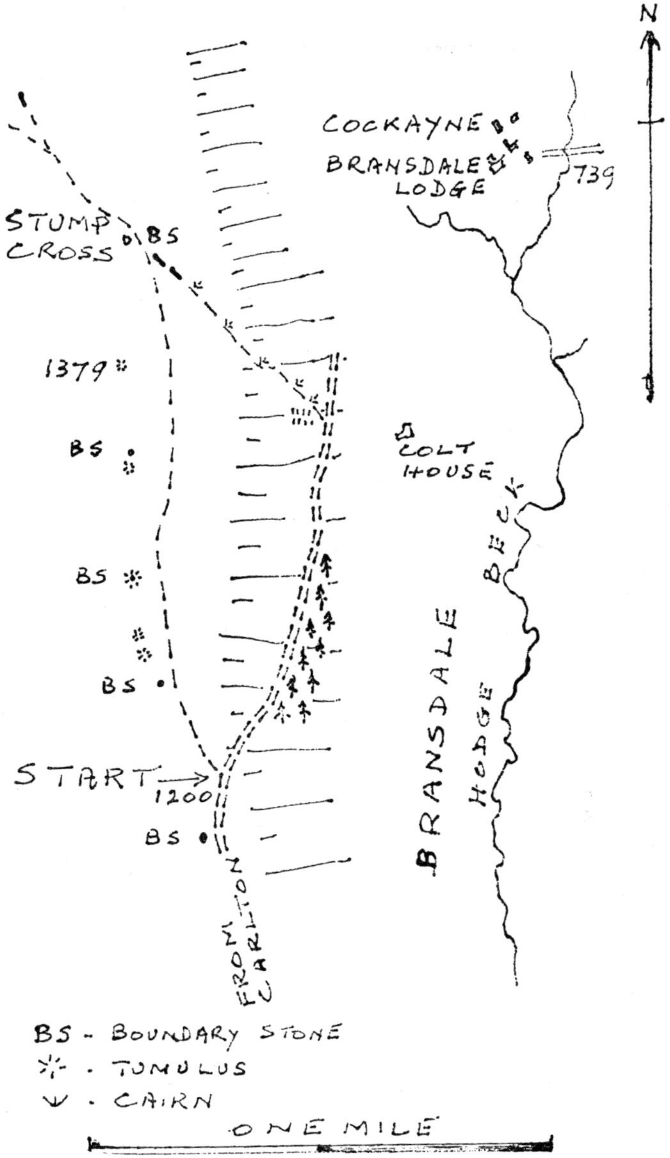
N
COCKAYNE
BRANSDALE LODGE
739
STUMP CROSS
BS
1379
BS
COLT HOUSE
BS
BS
START
1200
BS
FROM CARLTON
BRANSDALE
HODGE BECK
BS - BOUNDARY STONE
TUMULUS
CAIRN
ONE MILE

WALK 21

regular intervals are bumps and stones of various shapes and sizes; some are tumuli, others boundary stones and others combinations of both. Those interested will find that all the cairns have been opened up. It was probably done during the last century when there was a spate of digging of these ancient burial mounds which, although originally erected in the Bronze Age, were often found to contain the remains of people who lived in later centuries as well as the original bones. After passing a line, left and right, of stone shooting butts camouflaged with bilberry, and more cairns on the left, past three upright wooden posts in fairly quick succession, note for future guidance a small stone cairn on the right about 150 yards further on and in another 60 yards Stump Cross is reached on the left hand side of the path. This is the base of an old cross which marked a corner of the parish boundary; well, not so much a corner as a slight change of direction. It is also near the junction of our present track with the path coming up from Colt House. Above the stump more stones have been built up to make the feature outstanding among the other stones on this part of the moor.

Just north of the cross the view really opens out. The footpath to Tripsdale bears to the left 300 yards further on and before turning back at the track junction let us have a look round.

The depression down to the left is Tarn Hole; the track swinging round to the west to Tripsdale goes on to Bilsdale, but Tripsdale is out of sight below the line of the moor. Parts of Bilsdale can be seen with Cringle Moor and Carlton Moor beyond. The bulldozed route to the north points to the white trig point on Round Hill at Botton Head at 1,489 feet above sea level, the highest point, well known to long-distance walkers. Over to the east are the moors above Bransdale, Farndale and Rosedale.

Return to Stump Cross and the cairn 60 yards beyond, now on the left. The path at the start is difficult to find but on reaching the cairn the next in the line of cairns can be seen and the path is clear from now on. At the end of the cairns the path dips into a short stretch of marshy ground but this can usually be avoided. Make for the left-hand side of a groove going down quite steeply where the track is of shale and takes a straight course downhill beside some old workings, down to the road where there is another sign pointing to Bilsdale.

Turn right up the road and walk for nearly a mile back to the car. The short grass by the side of the road is good for walking on and an opportunity may be taken to get a closer look at Bransdale. The view later becomes restricted because of a plantation of larch trees but it opens out again just as the walker is beginning to puff a little before reaching the car at the top of the hill.

Walk 22 Cockayne, Bloworth Crossing and the Rudland Rigg Road—$6\frac{1}{2}$ miles (10·5 km)

FOR a dry-foot walk, leading at an easy gradient to the high moors at a famous junction of two equally famous routes, one an ancient road and the other a disused high level railway track, this would be difficult to beat. Bloworth Crossing is now known to thousands of long-distance walkers every year: the old ironstone railway track at this point is utilised by Lyke Wake Walkers; people on the Cleveland Way reach this crossing from the west and then turn north; walkers on the White Rose Walk may follow the route of the Cleveland Way, or they may cut across the line of the boundary stones which may be seen from here to the north-west.

The outward journey is mainly on forest roads which have the advantage of providing a dry, clear track, and for the time being the disadvantage of the forest roads—that of giving the feeling of being closed in—is missing because the trees in many places are still well below the line of vision.

Cockayne is the centre of a small community at the head of Bransdale, hardly big enough to be called a hamlet, beautifully situated among trees and as remote from the bustle of the towns as anywhere in England. It can be reached from Helmsley via Carlton and Cowhouse Bank or from Kirbymoorside via Fadmoor. There is plenty of good car parking to the west of the stream at Cockayne; assuming you have driven from Helmsley it is on the grass by the roadside before reaching the second cattle grid; if you have come from Fadmoor it is just beyond the first cattle grid after crossing the stream.

Walk down to the bridge over the stream, Bloworth Slack, a tributary of Hodge Beck which is the main stream of Bransdale. This is a delightful spot among old trees of many varieties, worth a pause before climbing up the road until it bends to the right. Here go through the Forestry Commission gate on the left and take the track through the field towards the larch and spruce plantation where there is a gate to be opened and closed. This forest track will be followed for more than a mile. It emerges from the first plantation after only about 200 yards and goes through an open space of grass, bracken and sedge. Over to the left can be seen the valley of Bloworth Slack and Cockayne Ridge beyond, with its distinctive clump of fine deciduous trees at the end of the nab and a smaller group of pines above it. The road passes into the tree area again, climbing steadily at first but then

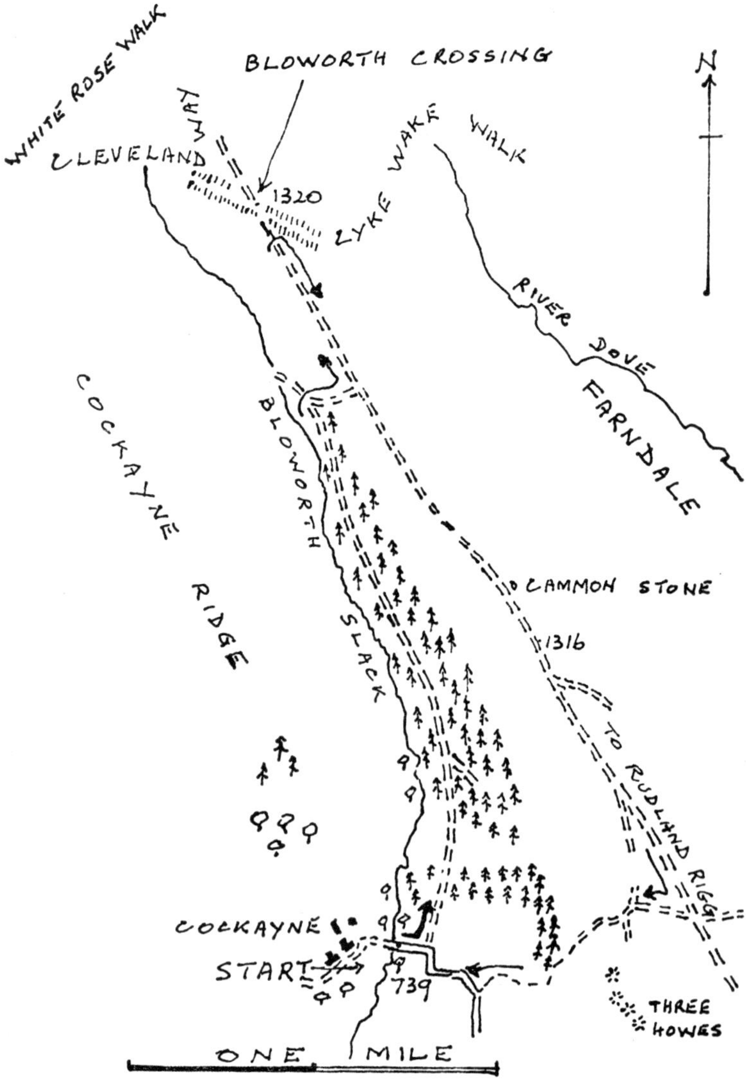
WHITE ROSE WALK
CLEVELAND WAY
BLOWORTH CROSSING
1320
LYKE WAKE WALK
N
RIVER DOVE
FARNDALE
COCKAYNE RIDGE
BLOWORTH SLACK
CAMMON STONE
1316
TO RUDLAND RIGG
COCKAYNE
START
739
THREE HOWES
ONE MILE

WALK 22

the gradient decreases. At first the trees are mainly larch; then there is an area of spruce. Across the valley another forest road comes into sight. It is, in fact, this same road which loops round at the head of the valley, but we shall leave it just before the loop. Before leaving the trees look ahead and if the weather is clear you should see some posts on the skyline at Bloworth Crossing and, possibly, some Lyke Wake Walkers.

Emerging from the trees, take the first turn to the right, where the road sweeps round in a hairpin, through a gate, and soon you will reach the top of the moor, passing a No Road sign on the way. Do not be apprehensive having used this road because, although cars are not admitted, careful perestrians are. Turn left at the T road for the diversion to Bloworth Crossing which can be seen half a mile away; we shall be coming back past this road junction later on.

The good stone and sandy track on which we are now walking is the Rudland Rigg road. Rudlang Rigg itself lies behind us clearly dividing Bransdale and Farndale. Five miles to the south, where our road leaves the Fadmoor-Bransdale road a signpost shows that Stokesley is 16 miles away and another one reads "Unfit for Motor vehicles". May it remain so for ever. These are heartfelt words. Many moorland roads have been "improved" during the lifetime of the author so as almost to be denied to the walker and the time has come to call at halt. Now that the area is a national park one can hope that this wish may become an expectancy. At Bloworth Crossing the owners of the site of the old railway line have managed to keep motor vehicles off it by putting a securely locked gate across it. The line, which linked Rosedale with Battersby and Middlebrough, carried iron ore across the moors to a height of 1,400 feet above sea level and was the second highest railway in the country. There is much to explore in this high country and the purpose of today's walk is to bring the reader to the crossing and after observing the routes, both ancient and modern, and perhaps some of the walkers on their long trails, return to the junction on the Rudland Rigg road which was joined half a mile away.

Walking south now, there will be observed on the left of the road at fairly regular intervals vent pipes with bright red covers, denoting the line of the North Sea Gas mains taking the gas northwards to Teesside. The good walking conditions underfoot do allow observation of the distant scene (as against the necessity on the rough paths on the open moor to watch every step in order to safeguard ankles and knees). Upper Farndale comes into view on the left and above it the twisting railway track contouring round the heads of the valley on Farndale Moor. On Westerdale Moor beyond, a depression leading away to the north shows the position of Esklets in the valley where are the gathering grounds of the streams forming the source of the River Esk, which finds its way to the sea at Whitby.

The distance from Bloworth Crossing to the turning off the Rudland Rigg road is a little more than two miles. Pass the junction with the forest track of the outward journey on the right and ahead on the left of the road will be seen the Cammon Stone, a big upright natural stone on the parish boundary, and when you reach it there is a mile to go before turning off. 200 yards beyond the Cammon Stone there is a green track to the left which is useful to take it if you want to have a closer look at the top end of Farndale, but continuing south one can see ahead to the right of the road the Three Howes on the skyline; in fact there is another tumulus nearby making four bumps in all. Keep on walking until you reach a green cross track just before the Howes and turn sharply right on to it, taking a backward glance into Farndale before leaving the area. The Lion Inn on Blakey Rigg should be seen over the valley and there could well be plenty of motor traffic passing it on the road.

So now the Rudland Rigg road has been left behind and the Three Howes are on the left. Soon the distinctive trees on Cockayne Ridge are in sight and the track makes towards them, broadens out and then bears left, becoming a narrow path by the side of a deep ditch which takes you to the left hand corner of the larch plantation below. Cross 60 yards of bracken on the path to a wall but do not go through the gap in the wall. Instead, turn steeply downhill on a good pathway through the bracken which leads into a deep groove and through a gap in the wall below into a field. Bear left, following the direction of the groove to the bottom left-hand corner of the field. Go through a gateway on to the valley road on which turn right, back to Cockayne.

Walk 23 Kirkdale and Sleightholme Dale -6½ miles (10·5 km)

HODGE BECK passes through three dales before it leaves the moorland area, first through Bransdale, then as it forces its way through the tabular hills it enters Sleightholme Dale and Kirkdale in quick succession. In fact the two are really one valley, separated merely by a bend in the river round the nab embracing Skiplam Wood. Both are well wooded; Sleightholme Dale is broader and more associated with the moorland.

Part of Kirkdale is just outside the National Park but it is famous for three things: St. Gregory's Minster, a cave and wild lily of the valley.

The little church dates from pre-Conquest times; particularly the sundial is of great interest. But whether or not you are interested in architecture you will certainly be charmed with the setting of this lovely church in the valley.

If you approach Kirkdale from Kirbqmoorside, take the Helmsley road; less than a mile out of town bear right off the main road; cross over the next road—a right and a left as shown at A on the map—and go downhill to the ford (which is sometimes dry) where there is also a footbridge. It is worth stopping here for a few minutes to walk half right from the bridge through the trees to the quarry where a cave was discovered in 1821 in which were the remains of lion, hyena, mammoth, rhinoceros and other mammals of former periods in our history. The cave can be seen high on the cliff face; if you are a climber and a caver you will be able to scramble up and see two passages through the two-foot high entrance. Proper equipment would be needed for a full exploration.

Park the car on the grass verge where convenient, but please note that the car park opposite the church is private, being for the use of congregations and visitors to St. Gregory's Minster. The walk begins here.

Go along the track to the left of the minster; keep by the wall side to a gate; cross the centre of the field to a good metal footbridge over Hodge Beck, quite a river when in spate but sometimes devoid of water; turn upstream after crossing and go along a track in a field with a larch plantation on your right. The stream is away on your left but you regain it at the far end of the field. Go through a gate into scrubland and climb a little on a wide green track up above the watercourse. As the track curves round to the right there is a gate on the left which pass through and take a track through the field with trees on both

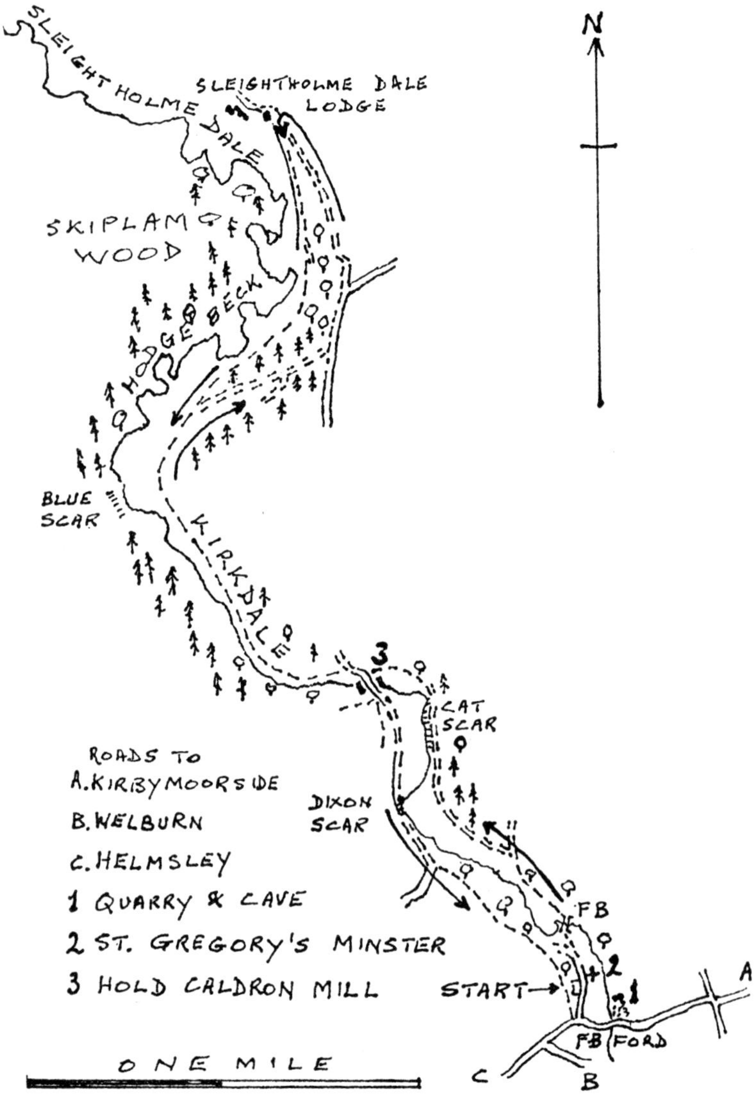

SLEIGHTHOLME DALE
SLEIGHTHOLME DALE LODGE
N
SKIPLAM WOOD
HODGE BECK
BLUE SCAR
KIRKDALE
3
CAT SCAR
DIXON SCAR
FB
2
START
1
A
FB
FORD
C
B
ROADS TO
A. KIRBYMOORSIDE
B. WELBURN
C. HELMSLEY
1 QUARRY & CAVE
2 ST. GREGORY'S MINSTER
3 HOLD CALDRON MILL
ONE MILE

WALK 23

sides, later cleared on the right. At a gate at the end of the field, take the track over the top of a crag (Cat Scar) formed by the sweeping action of the beck. At this part of the river there are sink holes in the limestone bed (as in Riccal Dale). For many months of the year the stream bed is dry below here to well below the start point of this walk. As you mount the hill over the scar you get a good view below of Hold Caldron Mill and Kirkdale. When you are nearly at the mill, leave the forest road and make your way towards it on a single track through newly planted beech and spruce trees. On passing through a gateway you will read a notice saying "Private, No camping, No picnics". Do not be alarmed, it does not say "No Walking" and you have been on a right of way. Similar notices will be read at points along the valley but the route has been carefully chosen. Years ago this was a favourite camping spot for schools and scouts.

At the mill you enter the National Park. It is pleasant to linger on the bridge and admire the local scene but we shall return to this spot and go over it later, so keep on the same side of the stream as far as another "Private" notice at a gate and go into the field on an undoubted right of way, a green track through the middle of it, until the field narrows, where you go through a gate into what used to be woodland, but at the time of writing only the stumps of the trees are left. On the right, a plantation of young mixed trees is beginning to grow. Then the path goes out into another field by the river, passes a gate on the right near the tall remains of a hawthorn hedge (note this for the return journey) and at the next gate on the right, near the end of the field there is a stile and another "Private" notice board. Go over it and turn left on a woodland track. On the right are newly planted trees; on the left are good open views of the wooded valley. As the road bears slightly to the right and starts to go up-hill, keep to the main track but look for a single track by the hedge which will be the point of egress on the return route. In the meantime the upward track through the trees rewards the effort by giving some fine views of Sleightholme Dale from time to time. Sleightholme Dale Lodge, the farthest point of today's walk, comes into view and is seen to be beautifully situated in the valley among trees.

At the top of the track at the edge of the wood, turn left on a working farm road which leads to a motor road, little used, on which turn left again to slope downhill through deciduous woods. Emerging from the trees you get glimpses of the moors higher up the dale, Birk Nab being the most prominent, and just before reaching Sleightholme Dale Lodge there is a sign on the left, by the side of a garage, which reads "Footpath to Hold Caldron".

Follow the direction on a good double track at the bottom of the wood. Below, the valley is wider; a footbridge over the river is inviting but do not go down to it, continue on the footpath by the woodside; climb a little, now into the wood, now immediately above the stream. Keep to the main track through the trees in spite of sighting another inviting footbridge below. The ground opens to a field on the right and the track becomes a single one when it reaches a young plantation, up-hill but soon down again towards a gate. Do not go through it, keep to the wood edge on the single track until you reach the forest road of the outward journey noted earlier. Turn right and you will soon be back at the stile you climbed earlier in the day to get on to this track, but for a change keep on this track through the woodland (cleared at the time of writing but planted again) until you reach the next gate on the right leading into the field near the old hawthorn hedge. One field, and the track is back into woodland again and by the side of the beck for a few minutes; out again past gorse bushes into the field which leads back to Hold Caldron Mill; pass a weir and go over the bridge.

From the mill the route is by the partly tarred road below the trees near the valley bottom, which takes you through a gateway and up-hill through the woods. Coming out of the trees, turn left off the road through the top edge of the wood as far as a gate. The right of way is by the edge of the wood on the field side. At the road at the far end, turn left and left again to bring you back to Kirkdale Minster.

The ramble has been more snake-like than circular and it was difficult to avoid the mile of duplication, keeping to rights of way, without reducing the quality of the scene. But there is always something new to see when reversing directions. As for the wild lilies of the valley, I have still to find them, but I am assured they are there.

Walk 24 Lowna and Birch Hagg-3 miles (5 km)

FARNDALE may be approached from the north via Castleton, from the south-east via Hutton-le-Hole and from the south-west through Gillamoor. All the roads are good for the holiday motorist but the best is the last one—simply for the benefit of the surprise view at Gillamoor. Before reaching the start point for the walk the motorist is recommended to park his car in the village and walk to the left of the church at the east end. The sight of dale and rolling moorland can be breath-taking. Time and time again the author has visited this spot, never failing to read the inscription on the church yard wall near the conveniently placed seat:

Thou, who has given me eyes to see
And love this sight so fair,
Give me a heart to find out thee
And read thee everywhere. J. Keble

The bridge below is the starting place for the walk. Two roads go away from it, one to Hutton-le-Hole and the other a rough short cut up the moor to the main Castleton road, called Lund Road. Looking down from the surprise view, the route of the proposed walk can be seen—up the dale through the woods on the east side of the River Dove; on to the moor as far as the Castleton road and back by Lund Road.

Motor down Gillamoor Bank, over the bridge and park where the roads fork. There is room for many cars here but there is a car park at the other side of the river, if preferred. Walk up the rough road for less than 200 yards where on the left you will see a notice showing the way to a public path to Low Mill. Take this path to a gate at the edge of the trees. This is Birch Hagg Plantation. On the other side of the gate, take the lower road through the trees, going upstream all the time but not immediately by the side of it. Emerging from the trees, the track reaches stream level at a clearing. If you happen to be here in mid- or late-April there will be daffodils in most places by the river, but the walk is a good one at all times. Birch Hagg bridge on the left is a good strong one but instead of crossing the river, continue in front of Birch Hagg House in accordance with the direction of a signpost just before it, showing the way to Low Mill.

The clear track continues through more woods, a clearing on the right, then more trees left and right. Keep to the left at the fork ahead until you reach a wall where turn up to the right as far as a gate and out of the woods into a field where a green track leads to Hagg End Farm. If you want to go on to Low Mill the path goes straight ahead but in order to make the excursion into a round trip, turn up-hill on the farm road. Looking up the valley from this road, the sight is very fair. West Gill is at the end of the range of vision, backed by Horn Ridge. Soon after leaving the northern end of Birch Hagg Plantation, the road from Hutton-le-Hole to Farndale is reached. Cross straight over it and go forward on a green double track, first through bracken and then heather. Only a narrow strip of moor is to be crossed here, known as Pricket Thorn; upwards to the left it leads to Blakey Ridge. Should there be a shooting party on the moor it will be noticed immediately, in which case turn right on the road towards Hutton-le-Hole for a third of a mile and re-join the route at the first cross roads.

Assuming one has crossed the moor over the green track, turn to the right on reaching the main highway and walk by the side of the road for 250 yards on a good marging of cropped grass—much needed by the walker because this road over Blakey Ridge is a busy one. As you walk you will see ahead on your left two upright stones. The first and bigger one has been very clearly carved in the distant past with hands pointing the way to Kirbymoorside (Lund Road being the former main route to Kirby), Pickering, Malton and Gisbrough. The stone further east is much plainer and is a boundary stone with a name—Thorn Stone—bearing only the initials T.D., "D" standing for Darley, the name of the Lord of the Manor. From here there is a view of the valley of Hutton Beck; among the trees below is Spaunton Lodge and the moor beyond is Hutton Ridge.

Return to the main road and take the gravel road, Lund Road, almost opposite the stones. Soon the motor road is reached, the one which was crossed a third of a mile away to the right; cross it and continue downhill on Lund Road which now takes on a more stony character. 1,200 yards further on and you are back at the car.

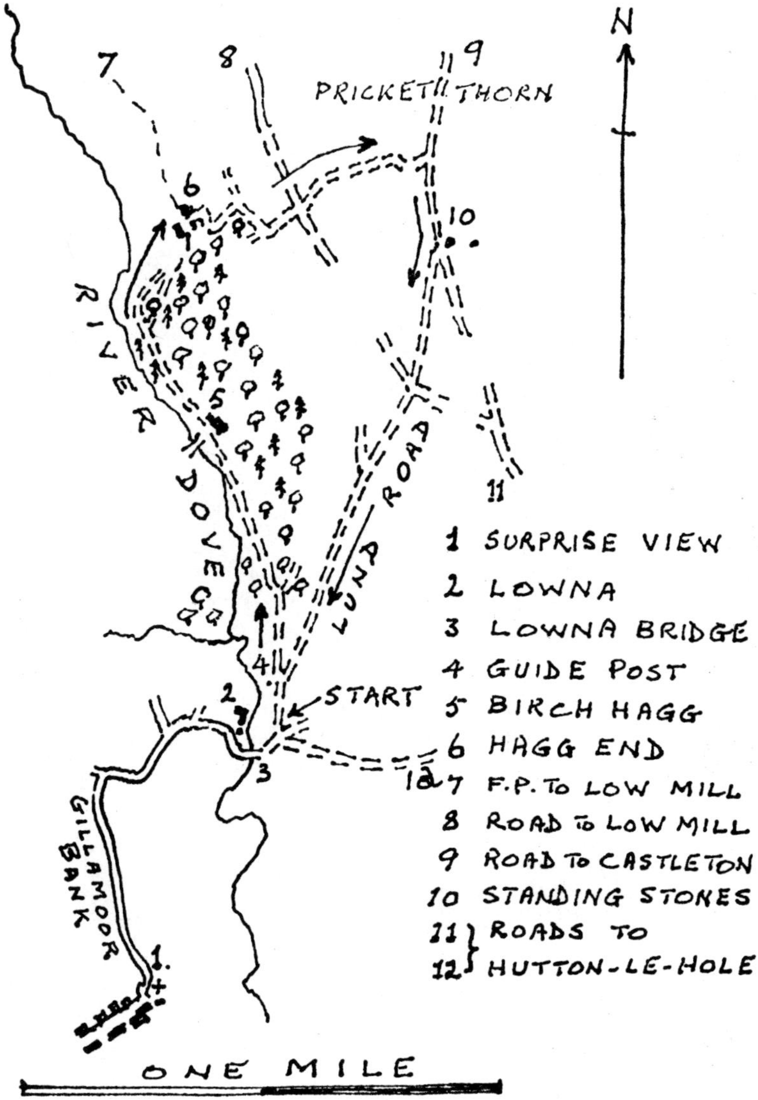
N
7
8
9
PRICKET THORN
6
10
RIVER DOVE
LUNA ROAD
5
11
4
2
START
3
12
GILLAMOOR BANK
1.
1 SURPRISE VIEW
2 LOWNA
3 LOWNA BRIDGE
4 GUIDE POST
5 BIRCH HAGG
6 HAGG END
7 F.P. TO LOW MILL
8 ROAD TO LOW MILL
9 ROAD TO CASTLETON
10 STANDING STONES
11 } ROADS TO
12 } HUTTON-LE-HOLE
ONE MILE

WALK 24

FARNDALE

Walk 25 The Farndale Daffodil Route -3miles (5 km). And an extension on to Rudland Rigg and into West Gill-7 miles (11 km)

FARNDALE is lovely at any time of the year but the best time to visit it is when the famous wild daffodils are in full bloom, spreading a yellow carpet on the valley bottom and alongside the streams. Depending on the seasons, usually the most rewarding time to see the daffodils is from the middle to the end of April and although the blooms are spread all along the River Dove, the classic route for walkers is between the villages of Low Mill and Church Houses, the first one and a half miles of today's journey. For those who only want to stroll, stand and stare, to return by the outward route will present no hardship but there will be some, looking for more exercise, who will welcome a visit to the moors and the subsequent drop down to West Gill, a peaceful place.

Low Mill is a little more than three miles up the dale from Gillamoor and a little less than four from Hutton-le-Hole, and the free car park is in the centre of the village. At the height of the season, especially on Sundays, the car park soon fills up but the owner of the adjoining field opens it to motors at a small charge.

From the free car park take the track signposted to the daffodils, across the field and down to a footbridge over the stream. Turn left and you are immediately among the flowers which, as will have been read on the Nature Reserve signs, must not be picked. The river is quite wide at this point and on the whole of the daffodil route the path is on the east side of it, well marked by constant use and supplied with good stiles and footbridges all the way. The footbridges are needed only to cross the side streams. If occasionally you look up instead of down, you will see High Blakey Moor ahead, with Potter's Nab above Church Houses. When you have walked, strolled and loitered for a mile and a half you will reach the buildings of High Mill and this is the limit of the flowers for the time being. You could turn back here or go along the lane to Church Houses.

If the intention is to do the whole walk, turn left on the motor road opposite the Feversham Arms, signposted to Farndale West Side; it is busy in the season but there is only half a mile of it to walk on before the junction is reached at the top of the hill. Turn right and pass through a gateway immediately above Monket House; straight away turn left through another gateway on to a green track which rapidly rises through crags and becomes stony, justifying the sign at the bottom gate which reads "Bransdale Unfit for Motors". Continue on this good walking road until the cross road of Rudland Rigg is reached. Ahead to the right front will be seen one of the Three Howes which were passed on the other side in Walk No. 22. Straight ahead, beyond Bransdale and Bilsdale, there is the ever-present

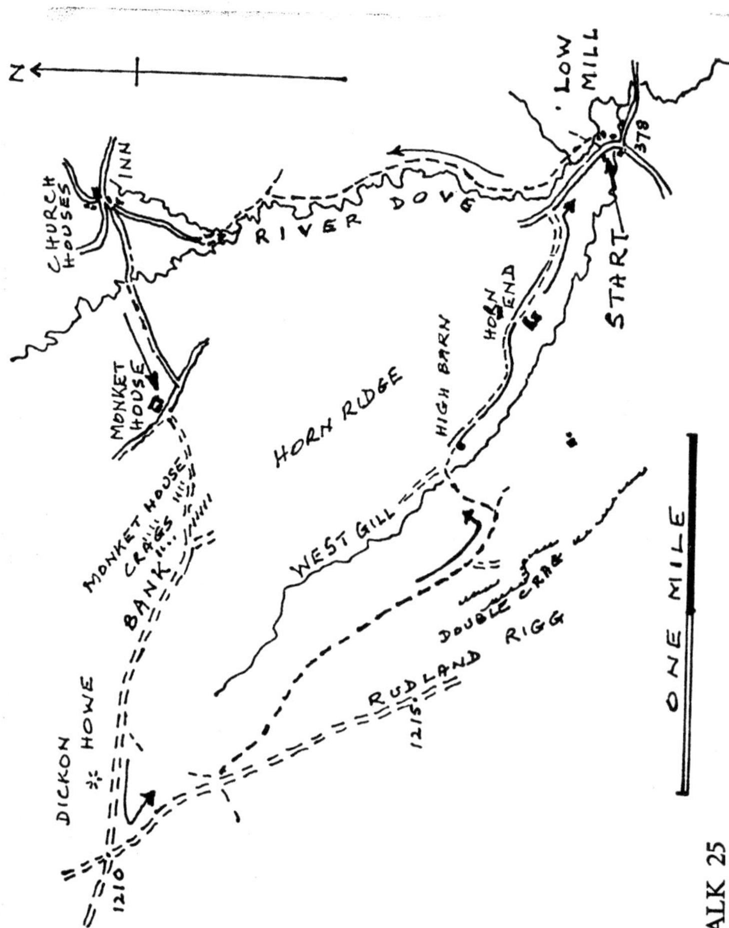

WALK 25

TV mast. There should be a guide post at this junction but when last seen the post was there but the signs were missing. Turn sharp left here, taking the Rudland Rigg road for half a mile, first bending to the left, then to the right on this road which is on most of its length as straight as an arrow. To the left there are views across Farndale to Blakey Ridge where on a clear day the inn can be seen and the road leading up to it from Church Houses. Nearer, there is Horn Ridge and dipping down on this side of it, West Gill, our next objective.

Approaching another finger post, look over the moor to the left to see the line of the bridle road into West Gill which is not always easily seen on the ground. The signpost reads "Bridleway to Low Mill". Take it and soon you will find yourself on a much better track leading to some shooting butts on the left. If you follow it do not descend beyond the fourth butt because the ancient track runs parallel to the stream below until it nearly reaches the crags, which will soon be seen ahead, where it slants down below them on to some bumpy ground, sometimes along little ridges, sometimes in the hollows, with the crags, now above and to the right, never far away, until a wall is reached. In the springtime the path is fairly easily seen from above but when the bracken is high one has to keep a sharp look out for it. Looking down into the valley below, one can see a barn at the other side of the stream, beyond some trees; the next objective is a footbridge 200 yards upstream from the barn (High Barn) and to reach it the track bears left, through a gate and the field below on the left.

The plank footbridge is called Foul Pot Bridge. It has a hand rail in a somewhat rickety condition and the boards can be slippery in wet weather, so cross very gingerly; in fact it is good to know that 300 yards upstream there is a concrete cattle bridge (at the top end of the field) and, somewhere between, the beck is narrow enough to stride across. Turn right over the stream on to a cart road which passes the barn and some gates, at least one of which will probably need to be opened and closed. The beck drops away to the right on the other side of a wall and the track passes through the middle of a field and to the left of Horn End Farm. A good farm road goes down to the narrow motor road below; at the junction a signpost reads "Bridleway to Rudland Rigg".

Turn to the right on the road; looking down through the trees, the River Dove will be seen and the daffodils first noticed on the outward route. There were no daffodils in West Gill but it is nevertheless a delightful place of pastoral peace—often in marked contrast to the wind and ruggedness of the surrounding moors. 600 yards of road walking brings one back to Low Mill.

Walk 26 Farndale-A Dale End Walk-2½ miles (4km)

SOMETIMES it may happen that on arrival in Farndale the daffodils are beginning to fade, either because of an early season or because one is just too late in getting there! It is therefore comforting to know that higher up the valley the flowers bloom later. The walk now being suggested takes one to both sides of the dale at the top end and when crossing the river both ways one comes across some lovely little corners among trees bearing their mass of daffodils. As in the rest of Farndale, there is really no out-of-season for this country, lovely at any time, beneath the moors. The only up-hill work to speak of will be seen from the car before setting off.

Go by car to Church Houses and continue on the road sign-posted "Dale End Only"; it leads to the top end of the valley on the east side. Soon, looking down to the left you will see the beautiful part of the dale in which it was proposed to build a reservoir. The arguments for and against had been going on for very many years until at last the conservationists felt that parliament had made the right decision and the battle had been won. But the water authorities still fight on; may the battle always be only of words! The narrow road above Church Houses takes us about two miles further up the dale before reaching Esk House where there is a sign on the left denoting a public footpath. Note this as you pass it, as this is where you will emerge on to the road on the return journey, and continue by car up the steep hill, beyond which there is plenty of car parking space by the roadside. Or you may prefer to find a spot to leave the car before going up the hill. The only difference that decision would make to the walk would be to bring the walk up-hill on the road to the beginning of the day instead of the end.

Now continue up the road on foot. There will be very little traffic to disturb you, for the tarmacadam ends half a mile further on; you will have plenty of opportunity to admire the views of the head of the dale. The road curves to the right and downhill and at the bottom is Gill Beck; this is quite a beauty spot. Now you must cross the bridge over the beck to a sign-post pointing up the valley which reads "Bridle Road to Bloworth". Opposite the sign is a green lane leading down to the river. Take it and soon it will take you over the beck again, through a gate at the bottom and on a good stone footbridge over the River Dove. You may wish to linger in this pleasant

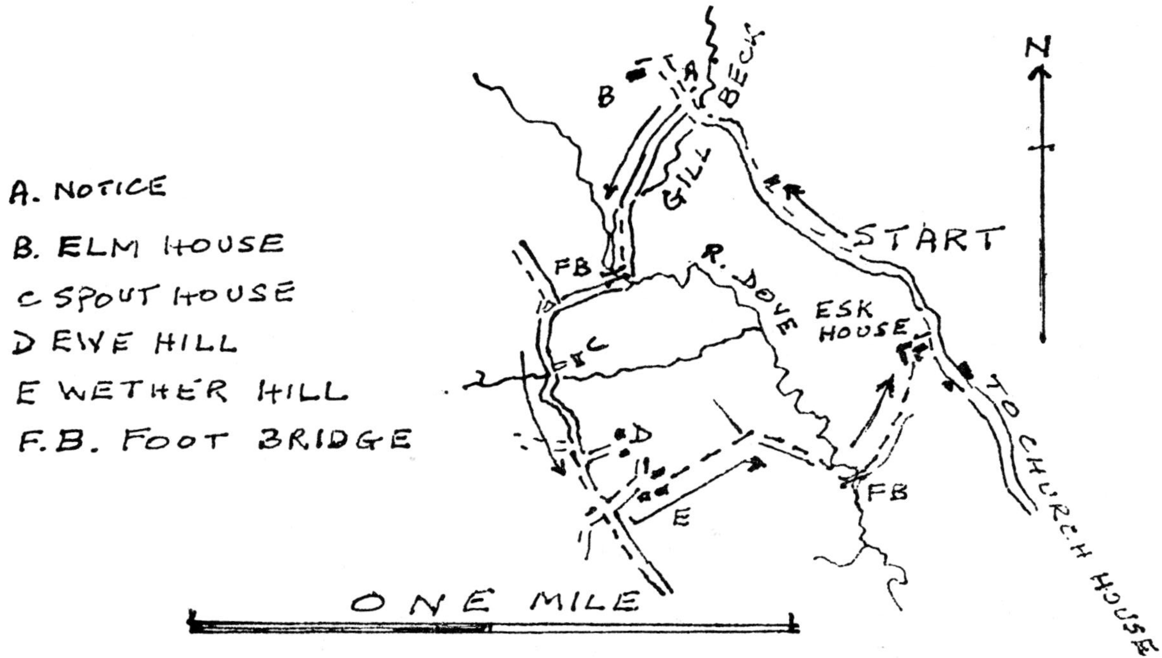
A. NOTICE
B. ELM HOUSE
C SPOUT HOUSE
D EWE HILL
E WETHER HILL
F.B. FOOT BRIDGE
N
START
TO CHURCH HOUSE
GILL
BECK
R. DOVE
ESK HOUSE
FB
FB
A
B
C
D
E
ONE MILE

WALK 26

place among the trees before continuing along the lane up the other side.

At a green triangle a little further on, the road on the west side of the dale is joined. Here it is a rough track and just right for walking on; turn left and as you walk down dale you will see three farms on the left. Less than half a mile from the turning on to this road there is a gate on the left and a track leading down to the third farm—Wether Hill—where the right of way passes between the house and the buildings, beyond which there are three gates. Take the middle one into the grass field leading down to the river. Keep more or less to the wall on the left and go through a gap in the wall straight ahead; through a gateway beyond; bear right to a stone stile at the corner where a wall meets the river; over the stile where on the other side, in the season, there is a carpet of daffodils within a bend of the river—a good sheltered spot suitable for a picnic.

Cross a footbridge to the other side of the river to a track which goes uphill by the side of a little stream and then leaves it to cut across the field to the farm which can be seen on the left (this is Esk House) and join the motor road at the Public Footpath signpost seen before leaving the car. If the car was left over the brow of the hill, all that now remains is to walk up the hill on the road.

FARNDALE

Walk 27 Farndale to Railway Track and return by Gill Beck-5 miles (8 km)

THIS is a splendid excursion starting at 700 feet above sea level and giving two miles of easy walking at a height above 1,200 feet, taking in two lovely valleys, with fast-flowing streams, on the way. Walking conditions are very good, apart from some fairly marshy land near both stream crossings.

Take the car to the head of Farndale on the east side by turning up the road marked "Dale End Only" in Church Houses and continuing for nearly three miles, almost to the end of the tarred road. You will know you have reached your destination when you have descended a steep hill, passed over a stream (Gill Beck) and observed a signpost on the right "Bridle Road to Bloworth". Leave the car here on the grass verge and set off walking up-hill, for the intention is to follow the direction of the bridleway almost to its destination at Bloworth Crossing. Climbing the hill, you will notice on the right a Public Footpath sign. This is the point of return.

As soon as the road reaches Elm House at the top of the hill it ceases to be a motor road and you find yourself first on a rough cart track and then on a fine green road after opening, passing through, and closing a gate. The crags ahead are Middle Heads; we shall be passing below and to the left of them. A gate crosses the track before a ravine; go through it and down to the bridge below on the left; up on the other side, to the right of a post and wire fence; bear left with the fence; through a gap in a wall (two gateposts, no gate) and to the right of a ruined building. There is another building over to the right but do not go to it.

Having passed the ruined building you will find the track has now become a single path through the bracken, easily found and keeping to the right of a wall. Go over a hill and down to two gateposts at the end of a wall and descend to a patch of grass below. The ancient bridleway now sweeps down to the infant River Dove and crosses to a good track going upstream on the other side. If you have any difficulty crossing here it is good to know that upstream there are some stepping stones. A little higher the stream is narrow enough to stride across but the approach is rather boggy, and there is a scramble up the far bank to regain the bridleway ascending from left to right. The green line of the path can be seen going up through the bracken to a gap in a wall, a good place in which to turn for a good view of Farndale. Resuming the upward climb on a

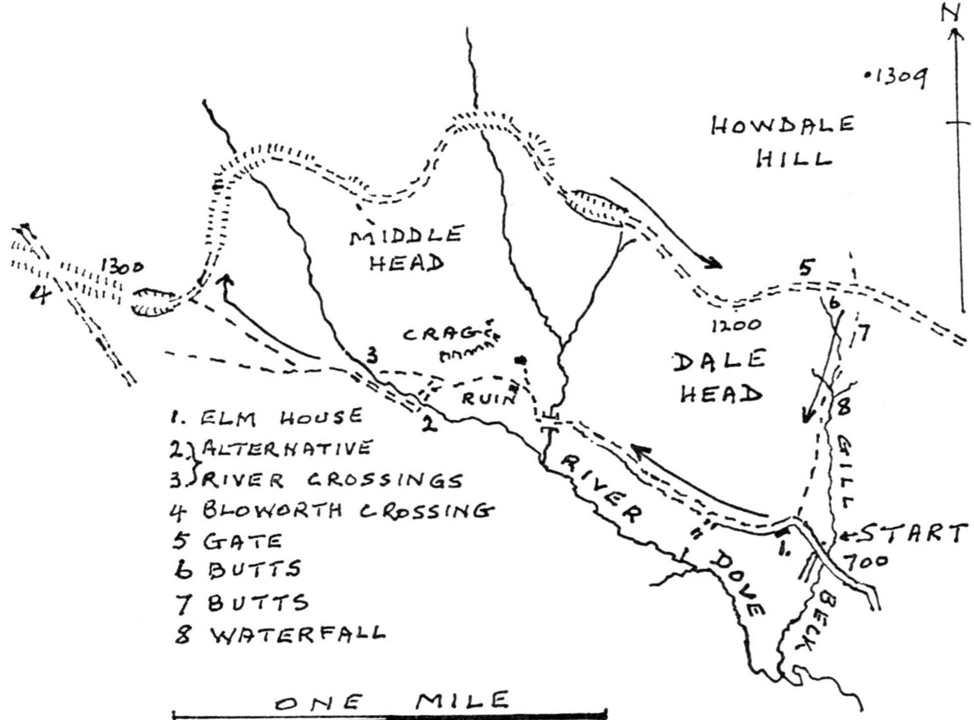
N
•1309
HOWDALE HILL
MIDDLE HEAD
1300
4
CRAGS
3
RUIN
2
5
6
7
1200
DALE HEAD
8
GILL
START
700
RIVER
DOVE
1.
BECK
1. ELM HOUSE
2. ALTERNATIVE
3. RIVER CROSSINGS
4 BLOWORTH CROSSING
5 GATE
6 BUTTS
7 BUTTS
8 WATERFALL
ONE MILE

WALK 27

path through bracken, the track bifurcates where the gradient decreases. The alternative straight ahead goes past some shooting butts from which the gate across the old railway track at Bloworth Crossing can be seen. But today take the right hand path which cuts across the head of a little valley and continues on multiple tracks as far as the old mineral line which, chiefly in the nineteenth century, carried iron ore from Rosedale to Middlesbrough.

Turn right on the railway track, now used by 6,000 Lyke Wake Walkers a year, good for stepping out and making up any lost time. There is no map reading to do for the next two miles. Notice the engineering of the high embankments, the cuttings and the curve of the line, contouring just below the tops of the moors. Looking right here and there, one is able to follow the route of the outward journey; on the left the rough peat hags show how tough the going would be but for the use of this old track. After Dale Head there is a gate across the track from which should be seen ahead on the right a line of shooting butts. At the gate, look for three trees standing singly down to the right; make for them to strike a path through bracken and rushes which crosses a small stream and leads to a well-worn path through bracken.

Looking back it will be seen that just behind and below the butts two streams converge and join the trickle just crossed over. This place is Gill Wath and the stream, Gill Beck, immediately plunges into a ravine below in a fine waterfall.

The path is now very clear between Gill Beck on the left and a dry dike on the right. It goes down to a gap in a wall and, still keeping to the side of the dike, passes to the right of another wall. Passing through a gateway you are now between two walls. Follow the one on the left on a stony track downhill until you reach the road at the "Public Footpath" signpost seen at the beginning of the journey, and you are less than 100 yards from the place where you left the car.

THE OLD RAILWAY ABOVE FARNDALE

Walk 28 Lastingham and Spaunton Moor -8 miles (13 km)

FOR a good walk with views of Rosedale and a fine moorland path home on a track well marked with cairns, this one takes a lot of beating.

The best approach to Lastingham is through Hutton-le-Hole, a famous moorland village of great beauty and possessing a fine folk museum which is rapidly becoming equally famous. Lastingham, too, is a pretty village in a lovely situation between Farndale and Rosedale. The church, built on the site of the monastery of Bishop Cedd, has a well-preserved Norman crypt and is outstanding in its many features of interest.

Walking begins in the centre of the village. Where the main road takes a sharp turn south for Lower Askew, take the road north for only a few yards. On the right there is a small patch of grass at the end of which is a stile, which can be seen from the road. Go over it (and look back for a view of the church with its fine apse) and pass between two hedges until a field is reached. (If this lane—a right-of-way—is impassable because of overgrown bushes, go straight up the road to the gateway leading to the moor, with signpost reading "Bridleway to Rosedale", and follow the wall round to the right.) Immediately take a diagonal turn up-hill, aiming for a stile.

When you have crossed this, you must continue diagonally through the next field, pass a clump of trees and go over another stile to the right of the field corner. Keep to the top side of the next field and go through a gap in the hedge; continue upwards to a gateway, keeping a wall on your left. Go through a gate at the top of the field; go forward for a few yards and turn right on a clear track on the edge of the moor, through bracken and a little heather. Now the track slopes downhill to some stepping stones across Tranmire Beck, uphill passing a hawthorn tree through bracken and then by the side of a wall, crosses a clear, wide moorland track (grassy) and almost immediately reaches a stony track. Turn left on this and you will have open moor on your left and a hedge on your right, through which you will see Rosedale below and Cropton Forest on the other side with Cropton church to the south of the forest.

Very soon the isolated farm of High Askew comes into sight and when the road reaches the gate a field away from the farm-house turn left on the single track on the left hand side of the wall. On reaching the end of the wall the line of the right of way is straight ahead (a projection of the line of the wall) but for the next half mile the path is not always visible. If, however, you pass two thorn trees just beyond the end of the wall and get on to a double track which leads up-hill to the left of two birch trees seen ahead near the skyline, then make for the two trees, you should pick up the path in a shallow dike which should be seen ahead making slightly to the left of two houses, now visible (Hartoft End). The dike, with the path sometimes in it, sometimes by the side of it, become more pronounced as you go along, keeping fairly level. Before coming opposite the houses you should notice a road bridge on the right down in the valley and hereabouts the single track links up with a double track coming down from the moor on the left and from now on the forward trail is unmistakable. When opposite the second house on the other side of the river—the white one which is the inn at Hartoft End—the path keeps more or less parallel to the stream, and the road beyond, at distances not less than 150 yards from the water. Keep to the left of an intake wall where our track is joined by another coming up from the river, and keep to the left of another wall, this time enclosing a wood, and you find yourself going up-hill. There are steep crags on the left, Cumratph Crag, but no prize is offered for the correct pronunciation!

After passing through some tree and scrub land you will find that the path leads to a gate before Hollins Farm. Go through it, pass Hollins Farm and into the lane which goes up the dale to the inn. Turn left on the tarred road and ascend Rosedale Bank at a gradient of one in three in places. There is much to see on reaching the top. First, there is a good view of Rosedale with the village of Rosedale Abbey below. Next, take a look at the many remains of the old nineteenth century industrial life connected with the iron mines—the railway terminal, the old buildings and what remains of Rosedale Chimney which, until it was demolished in 1972 for the sake of safety, was a landmark for many miles around on the moors and in the Vale of Pickering.

At the top of the hill on the left hand side turn off the road on a path by the side of a concrete hut. Now the direction is south all the way to Lastingham over Spaunton Moor. The first feature is Ana Cross, sometimes known as One Howe Cross, well preserved, with three arms of the cross at the top all cut from the same stone. It is in place of the original, old maps showing the location as merely being the site of the cross. The remains of the original are now in Lastingham church.

There are several paths near the cross; take the one which passes to the right of it, following grooves and depressions which typify tracks of ancient origin. Soon a clear single track goes past a series of cairns which undoubtedly help to define it.

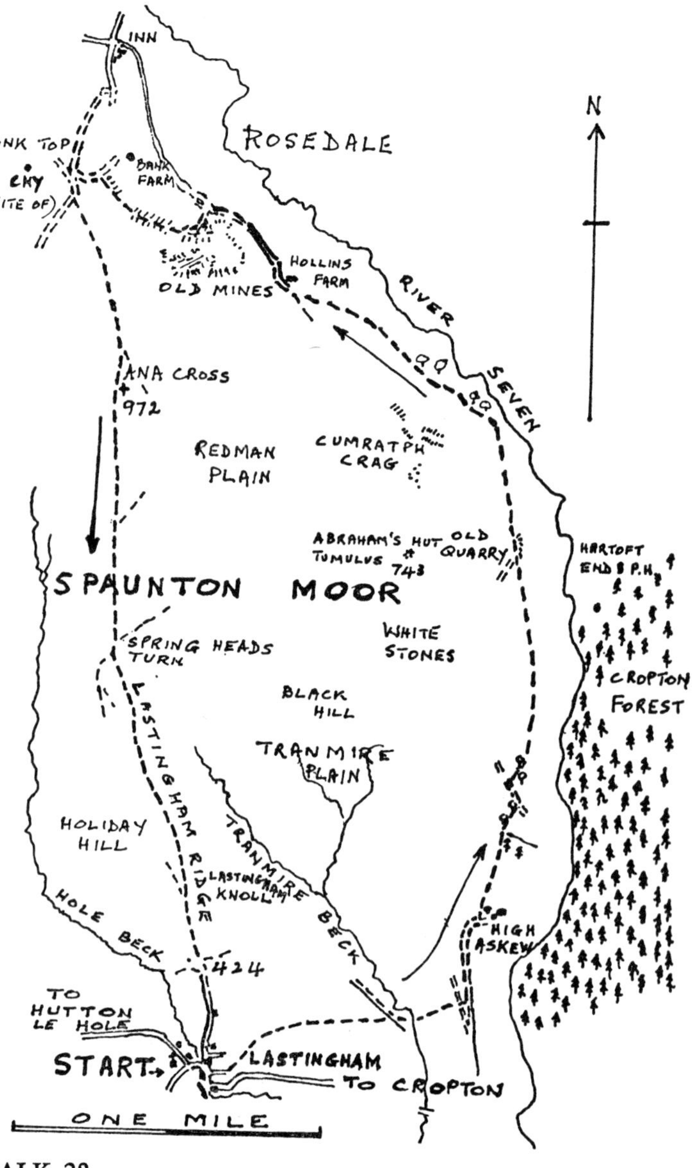
INN
ROSEDALE
N
BANK TOP
CHY
(SITE OF)
BANK FARM
HOLLINS FARM
OLD MINES
RIVER
SEVEN
ANA CROSS
972
REDMAN PLAIN
CUMRATPH CRAG
ABRAHAM'S HUT
TUMULUS
743
OLD QUARRY
HARTOFT END P.H.
SPAUNTON MOOR
WHITE STONES
SPRING HEADS TURN
CROPTON FOREST
BLACK HILL
LASTINGHAM RIDGE
TRANMIRE PLAIN
HOLIDAY HILL
TRANMIRE BECK
LASTINGHAM KNOLL
HIGH ASKEW
HOLE BECK
424
TO HUTTON LE HOLE
START
LASTINGHAM
TO CROPTON
ONE MILE

WALK 28

The marking of tracks by means of cairns is more reminiscent of Lakeland than the North York Moors where cairns usually mark old burial mounds. Look out for footpaths leading away from the main track which keeps to the ridge developing to the south. Eventually a double track is reached and shooting butts will be seen on the right—on Holiday Hill. On the left is Lastingham Knoll; straight ahead is a seat, beautifully situated above the village and giving fine views of the tabular hills which help to enclose it.

The gate below the seat leads to the road which was left at the beginning of the day's walk.

ANA CROSS

Walk 29 Rosedale and Northdale-2½ miles (4 km)

ROSEDALE ABBEY is a lovely little village situated at the confluence of the River Seven and Northdale Beck. The name of the village can be confusing because there is no abbey standing there, although a few fragments of a twelfth-century nunnery can be seen near the church.

Up the dale from the village are two very fine conical hills within the valley, each surmounted by a clump of conifers. The stroll now being suggested takes one up the main valley by the side of the River Seven for a short distance; cuts across to Northdale by way of a route between the two knolls; then beside Northdale Beck, returns to Rosedale Abbey. Northdale is a secluded, peaceful spot in which to linger.

The best approach to Rosedale from the south is via Pickering, Wrelton and Cropton. If coming from Kirbymoorside, avoid the direct approach via Hutton-le-Hole and the three in one gradient of Rosedale Bank near the site of the now demolished Rosedale Chimney. The approaches from the north via Castleton or Egton Bridge are quite reasonable for the motorist although the gradients are steep here and there, especially on the Egton Bridge road via Hamer House (a ruin well known to Lyke Wake Walkers).

Park in or near the village and look for the caravan site up-stream from it by the side of the River Seven. Make sure you get the right one—there are two others not far away. Fortunately all three sites are well hidden so as not to make too much of an impact on the general scene. Our start point is from a side road to the west of the parish church and the central road through the site leads quickly to the river. There are some good footbridges across the stream but today's walk keeps to the right hand side of it (the true left bank) all the way until leaving it.

Do not immediately go down to the side of the river, go up a slight incline to a gate; on the other side still keep up above the water (the field below is marshy) until you reach another gate. Go through it and walk on the right hand side of a wire fence to another gate from which a track goes down to river level where there is first a stile and then a footbridge. Go over the stile but not the bridge and you find yourself among trees on a track which very soon goes up-hill. It can be somewhat muddy in wet weather but it becomes dry on reaching the top

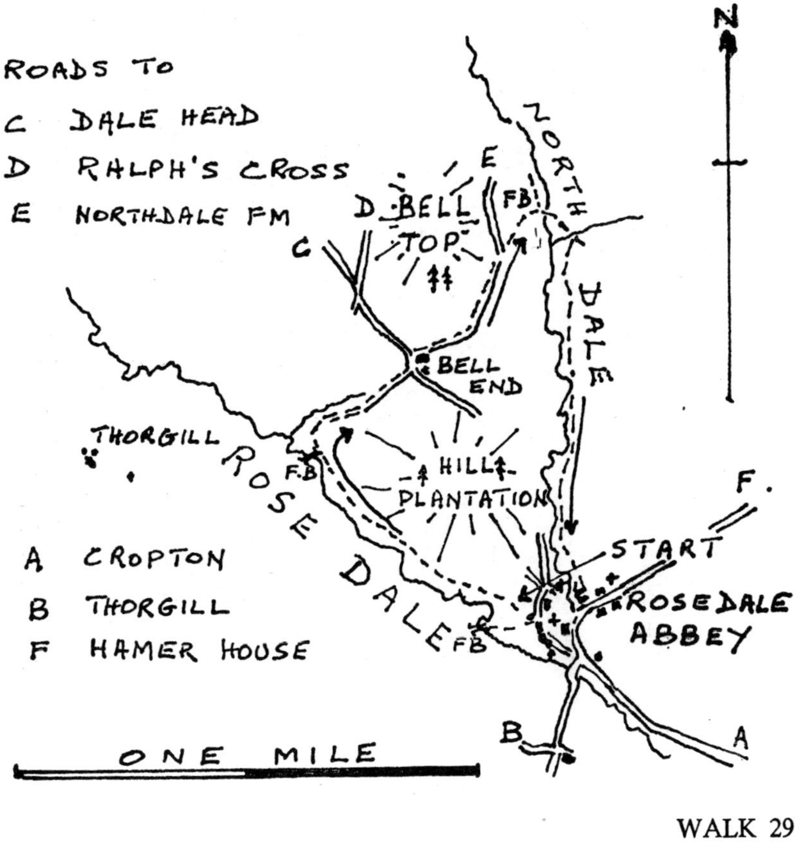
ROADS TO
C DALE HEAD
D RALPH'S CROSS
E NORTHDALE FM
N
E
D
BELL TOP
C
FB
NORTH DALE
BELL END
THORGILL
F.B
ROSE DALE
HILL PLANTATION
F.
START
ROSEDALE ABBEY
FB
A CROPTON
B THORGILL
F HAMER HOUSE
B
A
ONE MILE

WALK 29

where the path turns inland and is fenced on both sides, passing through broom, bushes and bracken. Looking ahead one can see the two knolls, Bell Top on the left and Hill Plantation on the right. Our road will take us partly up the side of Bell Top. In the meantime go through a gate at the end of the lane, on the cart track keeping to the left of a hedge and out on to a tarred road opposite Bell End Farm. Turn left and turn right as soon as the farm buildings are left behind, on to a metalled road which soon begins to climb a little and gives good views looking down the dale on the right. At a gate where the road begins to turn the corner of the hill you start to get views of Northdale. Soon you pass between two walls (no gate) and a small stream goes under the road from left to right. Ten yards further on take the green track down to the right.

The path goes past several walls and tracks, left and right, straight down to the delightful little beck, which cross by a grass-covered stone footbridge. Go through a gate on the other side and ascend the opposite bank, cross the field on the path which turns slightly right to a point about a third of the way up the boundary wall. Cross a small stream and go over a stone stile. Bear right and look for a gateway by a telegraph post near the stream.

Cross the next two fields to the obvious gateways ahead. From here the almost perfect cone below Hill Plantation will be observed, the green contrasting with the russets of the bracken on Rosedale West Side. Now the path is immediately to the right of a stone wall and the ground can be wet, but convenient stones are provided. It is a farm track which goes over a stream on a bridge. Bear left and go through two gates in quick succession. Then turn right and go diagonally across the field to an open gate near the beck and from now on the footpath keeps quite close to the beck through a series of fields, with gates, the last being a football ground. Bear right and go through a gate by the side of the beck and out on to the village road by a chapel, four garages and the car park for the Milburn Arms hotel.

Walk 30 Upper Rosedale-5 miles (8 km)

THE history of Rosedale is bound up with the making of iron. In mediaeval times the discovery of rich deposits of iron ore made Cleveland a centre of the industry; the monks of Byland Abbey made iron in Rosedale from the mid-thirteenth to the early sixteenth centries. But it was in the mid-nineteenth century that Rosedale became a centre of intensive industrial activity when the mineral railway to Battersby was engineered, for the transport of ore and iron blooms to the furnaces of Teesside. This went on into the early twentieth century. The scars are still there in the form of ruins of old buildings, pits and ovens but they have been mellowed by the passage of time and one is left with a romantic picture of the days when the valley teemed with thousands of workmen, some of whose cottages are still in use, many as holiday homes, nicely painted and well preserved.

It is the old railway track that offers the greatest possibilities for the walker. In Rosedale there are two tracks, the one from the east side contouring round the head of the valley to meet the west side track at Little Blakey. Quoting from the North York Moors National Park Guide No. 4, issued for the National Parks Commission and re-issued for the Countryside Commission, published by Her Majesty's Stationery Office: "The greater part of the track provides unsurpassed views into Rosedale and Farndale and a magnificent view across the lowland to Stokesley and beyond into the Tees Valley. This track should be preserved and kept in condition as a splendid moorland walk." To which the author adds "hear hear". Unfortunately in Rosedale itself, although the tracks are walked upon by hundreds yearly, they have not yet been established as rights of way; so today's walk will be on public roads and ancient rights of way, parts of which are little used nowadays.

Motor northwards from Rosedale Abbey up the dale towards Castleton for rather less than a mile when you come to a fork. Follow the left-hand road pointing to "Dale End Only" for half a mile and stop the car at the top end of two rows of cottages—Hill Cottages. There is room to park more than one car here without blocking the gateways; the gate on the right, by the side of a seat, denotes the end of the return journey.

Now continue on foot along the road, which at this point is

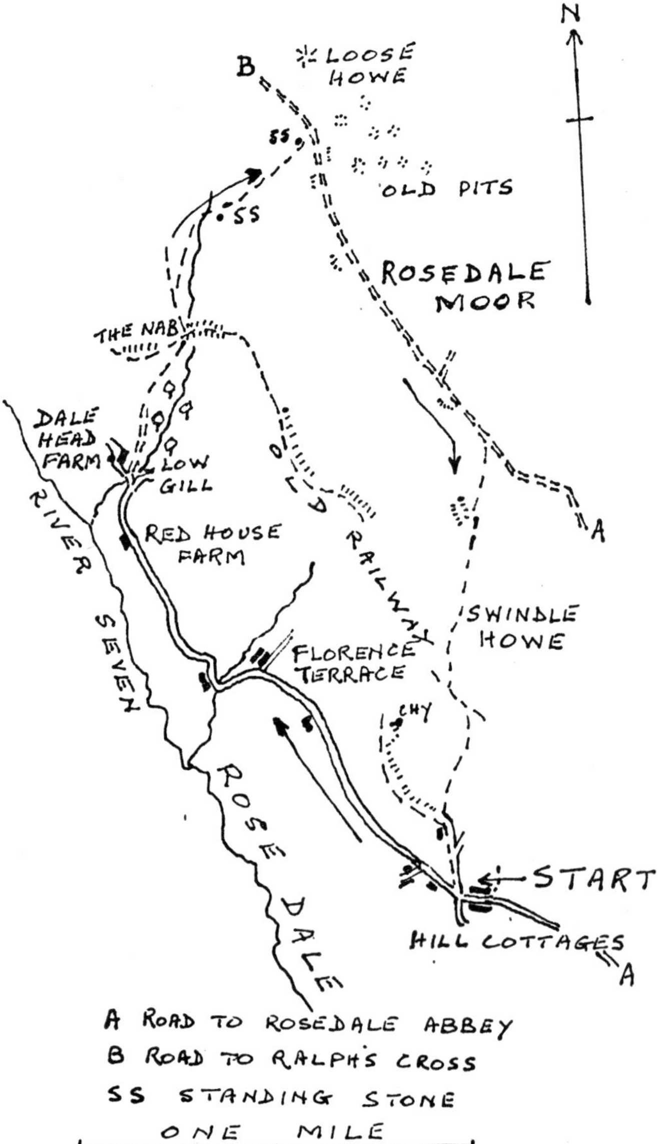
N
B
LOOSE HOWE
SS
OLD PITS
SS
ROSEDALE MOOR
THE NAB
DALE HEAD FARM
LOW GILL
RIVER SEVEN
RED HOUSE FARM
RAILWAY
A
SWINDLE HOWE
FLORENCE TERRACE
CHY
ROSE DALE
START
HILL COTTAGES
A
A ROAD TO ROSEDALE ABBEY
B ROAD TO RALPH'S CROSS
SS STANDING STONE
ONE MILE

WALK 30

still used by motors, but not often. The tracks of both railways can be seen on each side of the dale from here and on the right a fair number of disused buildings and ovens, also a chimney on the hilltop above the line. This is not so tall as the famous Rosedale Chimney, now demolished, but bear it in mind as a landmark on the return journey. Looking back on the other side is the village of Thorgill. Soon the dale becomes quite wide and is as beautiful as its name, dispelling any impression of gloom the reader may have gained by too much reference to its industrial past.

Pass Florence Terrace, a row end-on to the road; a farm house beyond a bridge and a sharp right hand turn; and soon you will see half a mile ahead Dale Head Farm and a green track going up from it to the railway track, our next objective. Meanwhile, looking to the head of the dale, you may see motor cars moving below Ralph's Cross, just beneath the skyline. This is the only part of the Lyke Wake Walk along a motor road. Pass Red House Farm where the tarred part of the road ends, and continue on the metalled road, which is a public unclassified road. The crag on the moors above Dale Head Farm is called The Nab; the route is to be in the dip to the right of it. On reaching the farm you should see a signpost on the right of the road, reading "Bridle Road to Great Fryup Dale". Follow the bridleway which goes immediately through a small gateway, on somewhat sticky ground, and keeps above the stream which lies on the right, on a well-defined path, much used by horses, through woodland at the edge of a ravine. As you begin to leave the tree area, if you look well over to the left you may see the Lion Inn on Blakey Ridge. Go through a small gate, still on a clear track through bracken, until you reach the old railway at the end of an embankment. To turn on it to the right would take you on a short cut to the "starting gate", but, sticking to the right of way, go straight across the track and up the left hand side of the ravine. As you near the top of the moor the path becomes less clear but nearing the source of the little stream near the head of the ravine you will see a standing stone. Stride across the streamlet to the stone. It has some old lettering on it but it is difficult to read.

Less than ten yards up-hill from the stone you will find the remains of an old trod in the form of a few substantial flat stones. Follow the direction of the stones on a slightly raised ridge (probably covering more stones) which can sometimes be seen and sometimes is obscured by heather and reeds. But on the skyline will be seen another standing stone, with a Howe to the left, behind it (Loose Howe) and the shale remains of an old pit to the right of it. (The shale heap is almost beside the road soon to be joined.) Lettering on the stone reads "Rosedale" on the near side and "Whitby" on the far side. The shale heaps thereabouts denote the position of coal pits long since disused. Half a mile down the road, 400 yards past a large shale heap on the right and 150 yards before the road ahead bears to the left, look for a roadside patch of grass on the right and a faint track through some rushes. Look for the chimney ahead, which you saw earlier in the walk and make towards it but slightly to the left of it. The right of way keeps to the left of an old quarry from which you will see a wall in front of you. Go down to it and follow its direction until you reach, first a stone wall intake and then a wire fence. Follow the fence down through rough pasture land, keeping the fence on your left until you are nearing another fence when you bear to the right and continue, now on a well marked track, on the right-hand side of the second fence.

White chimneys can now be seen ahead; just before reaching the chimneys you come to the level ground of the railway track where there is a gate on the left. Pass through into the lane beyond, which leads to the left of the white house (of the white chimneys) and on to the gate and the seat by the roadside where you left the car.

SOME USEFUL ADDRESSES

For complaints about obstruction of rights of way: The Clerk, North Yorkshire County Council, County Hall, Northallerton, Yorkshire DL7 8AQ.

National Park Information: The Information Officer, North York Moors National Park, Planning Department, County Hall, Northallerton, Yorkshire DL7 8AQ.

National Park Warden: Mr. R. Bell, Sutherland Cottage, Cropton, Pickering, Yorkshire.

The Forestry Commission, Bondgate, Helmsley, York.

Accommodation:- The North York Moors National Park Information Services does not publish a register of accommodation for the area. It does, however, supply a leaflet on caravan and camp sites and Youth Hostels and it recommends a number of excellent local guides (which contain accommodation advertisements), which can be obtained from:-

Ryedale District Council, Welham Road, Norton, Malton, N. Yorkshire YO17 9DT.

Hambleton District Council, The Old Vicarage, Northallerton, N. Yorkshire DL7 8DL.

The Yorkshire Naturalists Trust, 20 Castlegate, Clifford Street, York YO1 1RP. Nature Trail guides, including the Garbutt Wood Trail, may be obtained from here or from the Information Officer, N.Y. Moors National Park.

The Yorkshire and Humberside Tourist Board, 312 Tadcaster Road, York (Tel. York 707961), publish a guide which includes an accommodation list.

HELPFUL PUBLICATIONS

North York Moors National Park. Countryside Commission. 1969. (Official guide which provides an introduction to most aspects of study.)
H.M.S.O. P.O. Box 569 London S.E.1.

North Yorkshire Forests. Forestry Commission. 1966. (Also covers natural history, geology, geography and history of the Park.)
H.M.S.O., P.O. Box 569, London S.E.1.

Yorkshire Field Studies (Series 1). G. E. Bell. 1967. (Covers 51 field excursions of which five are in and around the Park.)
University of Leeds, Institute of Education.

Ryedale Country. (A useful local guide to Helmsley and surrounding villages.)
Ryedale Printing Works, Helmsley, Yorks.

A History of Rosedale. R. H. Hayes. (An interesting introduction to the area from prehistoric times to 19th and 20th century ironstone mining activities.)
Milburn Arms Hotel, Rosedale Abbey, Pickering, Yorks.

Ryedale Folk Museum Guide. 1971, (A guide to the exhibits which illustrate the activities of the old Ryedale communities.)
Ryedale Folk Museum, Hutton-le-Hole, Yorks.

Ryedale and the Vale of Pickering. J. H. Rushton. 1967.

Abbeys of Yorkshire. K. Wilson. 1969.

The Naturalists' Yorkshire. Yorkshire Naturalists' Union. 1971.

Railways in Cleveland. K. Hoole. 1971.

Whitby and Pickering Railway. D. Joy. 1971.
Dalesman Publishing Co. Ltd., Clapham, via Lancaster, Yorks.

Sutton Bank Nature Trail Guide.
Information Service, North York Moors National Park, County Hall, Northallerton, Yorks.

Exploring the North York Moors. Malcolm Boyes. 1976.
Dalesman.

LONG DISTANCE WALKS

Lyke Wake Walk. Bill Cowley. 1959. Dalesman Publishing Co. Ltd. Forty miles across the North Yorkshire Moors.

The Cleveland Way. Bill Cowley. 1969. Dalesman Publishing Co. Ltd. Yorkshire Moors and Coast Footpath.

The White Rose Walk. Geoffrey White. 1973. Dalesman Publishing Co. Ltd. From Roseberry Topping to the White Horse.

The Rosedale Circuit. Details of route from The Rosedale Circuit Secretary, Hawker Siddeley Aviation Ltd., Blackburn Welfare Society, Rambling Club Section, Brough, North Humberside. Send stamped addressed envelope.

The Crosses Walk. Malcolm Boyes. 1974. 53 miles over the North York Moors. Dalesman.

The Forest Walk. Reasty to Allerston. Details of route from The Walk Secretary, Forestry Commission, 42 Eastgate, Pickering, Yorkshire. Send stamped addressed envelope.

A Guide to the Cleveland Way & Missing Link. Malcolm Boyes. 1977. Constable & Co.